Double-talk on Weapons of Mass Destruction and Indian Security

Double-talk
on
Weapons of Mass Destruction
and
Indian Security

V.D. CHOPRA

GYAN

GYAN PUBLISHING HOUSE

NEW DELHI-110002

on behalf of

INTERNATIONAL INSTITUTE FOR
ASIA-PACIFIC STUDIES
New Delhi

Double-talk on Weapons of Mass Destruction and Indian Security
[Asia-Pacific Studies, Disarmament, History, International Relations, Politics.]

ISBN: 81-212-0612-2

Published in 1998 in India by
Gyan Publishing House
5, Ansari Road
New Delhi-110002

Laser Type Setting at: Computer Services, Delhi

Printed at: Mehra Offset Press, New Delhi

In Search of Vanished Blood

There's no sign of blood, not anywhere,
I've searched everywhere,
The executioner's hands are clean, his nails transparent,
The sleeves of each assassin are spotless.
No sign of blood: no trace of red,
not on the edge of the knife, none on the point of the sword.
The ground is without stains, the ceiling white,

This blood which has disappeared without leaving a trace
isn't part of written history: who will guide me to it?
It wasn't spilled in service of emperors–
it earned no honour, had no wish granted.
It wasn't offered in rituals of sacrifice–
no cup of absolution holds it in a temple,
It wasn't shed in any battle–
no one calligraphed it on banners of victory.

But unheard, it still kept crying out to be heard,
No one had the time to listen, no one the desire.
It kept crying out, this orphan blood,
but there was no witness. No case was filed.
From the beginning this blood was nourished only by dust,
Then it turned to ashes, left no trace, became food for dust.

Faiz Ahmed Faiz
(Translated by Agha Shahid Ali)

Contents

Contents

Preface

In this study an attempt has been made to objectively assess human suffering from the use of weapons of mass destruction—nuclear, chemical and biological weapons. In the post-Second World War period, the dropping of atomic bomb on Hiroshima and Nagasaki, chemical and biological weapons used in the 1960s and 1970s against the countries of Indo-China, Vietnam in particular, and the tragic developments in the Gulf countries, indeed clearly demonstrated that when scientific and technological inventions are used to serve political purposes, they lead to untold suffering of the people. The victims of these weapons and their children continue to suffer physically, psychologically and spiritually for decades. This aspect has been clearly established in this study. Therefore, as we stand on the threshold of the 21st century, a decisive movement towards the total elimination these weapons will determine the future of humanity on our planet. The international community has concluded treaties to eliminate weapons. Though these treaties standout as models for abolition of these weapons the harsh reality of the present scenario is that despite these treaties, stockpiles of biological and chemical weapons are being, built, though secretly.

The universally verifiable treaty to prohibit the production, possession, and use of chemical weapons globally came into force on April 29, 1997. There is already a treaty to prohibit biological weapons. Notwithstanding the existence of these two treaties, this study has established on the basis of objective facts, that the exponents of destruction of these weapons themselves have been promoting certain nations to acquire the capability of manufacturing these weapons. This is not a subjective estimate. It is based on hard facts, which cannot be challenged.

In the recent past, the third category of weapons of mass destruction, nuclear weapons has attracted attention. However, the most alarming development is that the exponents of elimination of these weapons continue to pursue a policy of helping certain states to acquire nuclear weapon capability. It is this contradiction between the declared objectives and deeds, which the peace-loving people all over the world need to recognise. The fact of the matter is that certain developed nations which have the monopoly of nuclear and other weapons are seeking to use their strategic superiority as an instrument to establish their hegemony over other nations, the developing and underdeveloped nations in particular.

There is no justifiable reason for tardiness and opposition to total elimination of all weapons of mass destruction, particularly nuclear weapons. While there has been an abiding desire and interest among the international community for total elimination of nuclear weapons, the reality also must be recognised that the focus and emphasis on nuclear disarmament that was so evident during the 1980s, is almost totally absent in the 1990s.

On the other hand there are encouraging signs of an increasing segment of strategic experts and former managers of arsenals of nuclear weapons who are forcefully articulating the desirability and the need for deep reductions followed by total elimination of nuclear weapons.

While this has yet to translate into policy, and could indeed take a long time to do so, we will be remiss if this trend is not taken into account. As of date, the only nuclear weapon state to unambiguously demand and commit itself to prohibition of nuclear weapons is China.

Nuclear weapons have no military utility. The military factor comes into play essentially to provide credibility into the posture and as a reminder of the possibility that they could be used resulting in a horrendous scale of destruction. Nuclear weapons really serve as powerful political instruments of coercion and demonstration of power, which are enhanced by the probability of threat and use of nuclear weapons. It is significant that compared to the one-time use of nuclear weapons, there have been 45 incidents when nuclear weapons were "used" as more explicitly a threat than the implicit threat existing in their very existence and possession.

The permanent extension of the Nuclear Proliferation Treaty (NPT) in May, 1995 without any unambiguous, leave alone binding, commitment to nuclear disarmament only reinforced the concerns that nuclear disarmament is not likely to be pursued by the weapon states in any meaningful way in the foreseeable future.

Jawaharlal Nehru once said that if ideas grip the minds of the people they become a material force. It goes without saying that all real changes in human history have come about as a result of force of ideas. It is necessary, therefore, to emphasise that elimination of all weapons of mass destruction will only be possible if the belief system and ideas that have sought to justify nuclear and other weapons of mass destruction are changed. This is precisely the purpose of this study.

The motivation for the author to compile this book came during his three visits to Hiroshima and two visits to Vietnam. During these visits the author participated in various seminars on the theme of elimination of weapons of mass destruction. There was something more to it. He met Japanese people who still are suffering from the explosion of the first atomic bomb, though their parents were the first victims. In Vietnam vast stretches of land cannot be cultivated even today because biological and chemical weapons were used to make them sterile almost three decades ago.

Today a nuclear war could destroy all living things on this planet. This warning, coming from scientists who have transcended their specific disciplines and nationalities, makes it clear that nuclear weapons are a kind of absolute evil. They must not be used for any reason; indeed, even their possessions cannot be condoned. The agonies of Hiroshima and Nagasaki clearly foretell the sinister consequences of nuclear war, and nuclear arms developments over the past 53 years make their abolition an inescapable conclusion today.

The tragic experience of people of Vietnam and the Gulf countries reinforces the argument that all peace-loving people in the world should unite to create a non-violent world free from all weapons of mass destruction, so that every nation and state can mould its destiny according to their choice. In this sense the world is on the crossroads.

This study, therefore, is a modest contribution towards the cause of building a new world order in which science and technology are put at the service for the betterment of the people and to give them a better life and not as an instrument of their destruction.

6.8.1998 **V.D. CHOPRA**
New Delhi

Introduction

In the post–Cold War period a sea-change has taken place in the international political environments, particularly after the collapse of the Soviet Union and liquidation of the socialist system in East Europe. This assessment is shared both by the exponents of the concept of "market economy based democracy" and those who still hold on to the theory that no stable international order can be build without conceptualisation of egalitarian societies. The question of disarmament and complete liquidation of weapons of mass destruction like chemical, biological and nuclear weapons is directly related to these conflicting doctrines.

War and Peace

With the ending of the Cold War there has been much discussion of the possibility of establishing a new world order that would bring about an era of peace. Unfortunately, while peace among the major states seems likely, the first major war of the new world order, the Persian Gulf War, occurred before the dust had settled from the collapse of the Berlin Wall. Iraq's build-up of chemical and biological weapons, if confirmed, was promoted in this period. How and why this tragic development took place has been tried to be analysed in this study.

Peace can be tentatively defined as the absence of large amounts of collective violence. This means that peace does not require the absence of all conflicts. There is no need to assume a harmony of interests in order to have a war-free system. It is not necessary to eliminate conflict, particularly disagreement, in order to have peace, but only to keep groups from trying to resolve their disagreements through the use of lethal violence. Of course, a deeper peace will be one that rules out even the possibility of the use of violence.

Given this definition, the problem facing the post-Cold War era can be intellectually framed in two ways. The first, is how to build a world system where the probability of war especially war among major states, goes way down. The second takes more of an interaction perspective. Here the question would be how to reduce greatly the probability that political actors will resort to violence to achieve their ends.

Territorial disputes can be viewed as an underlying cause of war in two senses. First, they are underlying in that they are not a direct or immediate cause, but rather produce a sequence of events that then result in war. Territorial disputes do not lead directly to war, but rather reflect a source of disagreement that encourages these kinds of interaction that result in war. It is the interaction sequence that produces war, not the territorial dispute itself. This implies that if these issues could be handled differently, then war would not occur. (Second, territorial disputes are underlying causes in the sense that if claims over territory are settled amicably between neighbours, then it is unlikely that any direct war will break out between them, regardless of other issues that arise in the future. Among neighbours territorial issues are the key to determining whether there will be a peaceful or hostile relationship. If these issues are resolved peacefully, then it is likely that the two will have peaceful relations for most of their history regardless of other disputes that may arise. In this sense, territorial issues have a causal force if they are settled non-violently. Territorial concerns, then, do not make war inevitable.[1]

In the post–Cold War period two parallel developments are taking place. It is necessary to take note of these developments to understand the problems connected with use of violence and new arms race.

Firstly, there is a growing tendency in Europe, which underlines that world politics and mutual relations can be conducted through dialogue and cooperation. The developments in the European Union and the G-7, now G-8 with the inclusion of Russia, are a clear manifestation of this trend.

Secondly, it is in the developing world that most of the armed conflicts have taken place in recent times either directly or through "proxy war". Kashmir, Afghanistan, Cambodia, Palestinian-Israel conflicts, Chechnya in Russia and in the Balkans particularly in Yugoslavia are clear indications of this trend.

A case study of all these conflicts shows that in varying degrees they were the outcome of moral and material support of outside powers. Let us leave this question at that and examine how these conflicts, as a matter of fact in almost all the conflicts, both during and after the Cold War had led to foreign interventions. These interventions show the international ramifications of these conflicts.

Of the 101 inter-state conflicts identified in the post–Cold War period, twenty-three of them were still ongoing in 1993. Furthermore, there was an upsurge in intra-state conflicts in the 1990s. When analysed for the type of conflict underway, 52 per cent were identified as ideological, 37 per cent ethnic; and 11 per cent were religious. Africa and Asia are clearly the most conflict-prone, each accounting for approximately 30 per cent of the interventions and 30 per cent of those conflicts in which there was no third party involvement. Europe accounted for 14 per cent of all interventions and 7 per cent of the conflicts with no interventions. Figures for the Middle East are 16 per cent and 13 per cent, and Latin America 13 per cent and 18 per cent.

In terms of interveners, 45 per cent of all interventions were carried out by major powers, 8 per cent of the interventions were under United Nations' auspices, and the remainder attributed to minor powers. The United States of America accounts for by far the most instances of interventions with 33, while the former Soviet Union and Britain were involved in eight and seven interventions, respectively. Out of the 118 cases of intervention only about 30 per cent were successfully considered.[2]

Most Frequent Intervening States	Number of Interventions
United States of America	33
United Nations	10
USSR/Russia	8
Britain	7
South Africa	4
Syria	4
France	3
Libya	3
Iran	3
Turkey	3
Afghanistan	3
China	3

These figures show that in the post–Cold War period there has been a sudden increase in the inter-state conflicts with resultant increase in the third party interventions, particularly by the United States of America.

In the academic parlance of a leading member of America's foreign policy establishment, the differences are so acute in the post–Cold War, period that they justify a macro-comparison in terms of "civilizations".

Cold War I was an ideological and economic conflict between "capitalism and communism." It is turning, Huntington argues, into a kind of Cold War II, a cultural conflict between civilizations. We may even, he hints, get a World War III along these lines. Indeed, the differences between civilizations and the awareness of such differences are seen to represent a significant new threat to the West. "More specifically the threat lies in any non-Western civilization that modernises without Westernising. Huntington cites a number of Confucian and Islamic states that he finds threatening in this respect."

From outside Huntington's Strategic Studies Institute at Harvard, these macro patterns are read very differently indeed. However, Asian commentators talk of a materially progressive, socially cohesive East, and of a West beset by crises of confidence and diverse communal disorders. They see the West itself, not some Islamic-Confucian connection, nor the modern day descendants of the Muslim and Mongol hordes, as being responsible for inter-civilizational strife. It is to the East, they say, that Westerners are now having to turn for positive examples of social repair. Westerners are urged not to act as if they were under seige, nor to close their mental gates on what they might learn elsewhere. Rather they are urged to "Go East, Young Man".

In an article with the above title the Permanent Secretary of Singapore's Ministry of Foreign Affairs notes, for example, the soaring crime rates, divorce rates, teenage suicide rates and declining educational standards that characterise liberal capitalism in the United States of America. Unlike the US, where liberating the individual has imprisoned society, East Asia still enjoys, he claims, relatively high levels of social order and family cohesiveness. Freedom in Singapore, he concludes, is not to be compared with licence that corrupts the West. It is rather the result of social order and discipline.

In an editorial on Asian values, an international weekly with a rather more global audience recently picked up the same theme. In a similar vein it waxed lyric about the deep differences between the West and Asia, not in values ....rather in the way their societies work. How societies work has a lot to do with the values shared by those who work in them, thus this distinction would seem more apparent than real.

The editors of the *Economist* are well aware that Asia contains 60 per cent of the population ... four or five major cultures, several distinct forms of social organisation, an ethnic mosaic of astonishing complexity, and three or four big religions. This would seem to make it more sensible, as they point out themselves, to talk about Confucian values.... Islamic values .... Japanese or Hindu values rather than Asian values per se. Given that Confucian, Islamic, Japanese or Hindu traditions are not monolithic, one would not want to stop there either.

Despite their manifest appreciation of this diversity the *Economist's* editors still can't resist sliding into the same simple dichotomy used by the Singapore spokesman. However, despite making all the appropriate disclaimers the editors of the *Economist* counterpose West and East just the way the Singaporean does.[3]

The Role of Asia-Pacific Region

Without going into Huntington's theory of "civilizational conflicts" and threat of World War III, one has to keep in mind that the centre of political and economic gravity has shifted to the Asia-Pacific region. This has changed the security perception of the developing nations and new power equations are emerging, as has been mentioned in this study.

It is in this background that new strategic doctrines are being evolved. In the final analysis the problem of elimination of weapons of mass destruction are related with it.

One of the key elements that will determine stability and future prosperity of the Asia-Pacific will be US policies towards this area. While it is far from being the sole superpower in the post-Cold War world, its military capability is awesome and with a global reach, its economy is the largest and Washington's political influence is by far the most significant.

After the end of the Cold War, US troop levels have remained steady at about 100,000 soldiers for the last three years. Compared to this its military strength in Europe decreased by about 20 per cent annually in the same period.

US economic involvement with the Asia-Pacific is even more substantial and growing. The total trade with the region amounted to 434 billion US dollars in 1994 or 37 per cent of total US trade. This was more than double of that with the European Union which was 17 per cent. US exports to the Asia-Pacific were 156 billion dollars in the same year or 30 per cent of the total. This sustains some three million jobs in the USA.[4]

The National Security Strategy of the United States in the post–Cold War period underlines the "growing importance of the Asia-Pacific to US prosperity". Assistant Secretary of State for East Asian and Pacific Affairs, Winston Lord, said before the Committee on Foreign Affairs in

June 1994 : "Asia is the key to the economic health of the United States and to the everyday lives of Americans. It is the most lucrative terrain for American jobs and exports. The 18 member states of APEC produce 14 trillion dollars worth of goods. Its exports were 1.7 trillion in 1993. The Asia-Pacific has accumulated 65 billion dollars in direct US investment. These are considerable US commitments and maintaining these will remain a high priority for Washington".

The US has been a strong supporter of multilateral arrangements in the region. It hosted the first APEC Summit in Seattle in November, 1993. It is a dialogue partner with ASEAN and is an active participant in the ASEAN Regional Forum (ARF). Security, enhancing mutual prosperity and building a new Pacific community constitute the three pillars of US policy in the Asia-Pacific.

US economic interaction with the Asia-Pacific is likely to grow at an even faster pace in the future. In the five years between 1987-92, US exports to every economy of the 17 members of the APEC increased by at least 50 per cent. East and South-East Asia remain an important market for US military exports. Foreign military sales in 1993 amounted to more than 10 billion dollars. The US has mutual security agreements with these five major countries: Japan, South Korea, the Philippines, Australia and Thailand. It is determined to see these arrangements continuing.

Following from the above, there are three major security challenges that face the USA. "Threats from Communism", no longer exist in the post-Cold War period. However, in the perception of strategic experts, the challenges to the United States are bigger than before.

There are now three main areas of concern to the USA.

Regional conflicts may be ethnic, religious, border wars or local conflicts due to a host of different reasons. Some may be apparent today. Many others remain submerged under the collective consciousness and may emerge unexpectedly according to American strategists.

Among these conflicts, North Korea has attracted the American attention because of threat to 36,000 US troops in this area. The Taiwan question may hot up though US-China relations are unfolding new trends. Other areas of concern are: the four islands in the Kurile chain between Japan and Russia, islands in the East China Sea between Japan and China, situation in Cambodia, and finally, the dispute over two islands between Malaysia and Indonesia. Now the American have begun to internationalise the Indo-Pak conflict on Kashmir. This shows deep American involvement in the regional conflicts.

The American policymakers are interested in promoting "Democratic structures based on market economy". This strategic objective has certain limitations. One need not go into them in this study.

However, the economic resurgence of the Asia-Pacific is not an unmixed blessing for the USA. The USA has enormous deficit in its trade balance with the region, not merely with Japan (approximately 60 billion dollars annually), China (30 billion dollars in 1994 and growing) and Taiwan but with some other South-East Asian countries as well. There is little chance of closing this gap early. Quite often efforts at opening markets are leading to major political difficulties.

US Defence Policy

This shows the broad direction towards which US defence policy is moving. This can be summed up as follows:

Firstly, the experts have identified four basic threats to America's security in the post-Cold War era. These are: (a) lingering nuclear threat from Russia and the Central Asian Republics; (b) the prospect of proliferation of nuclear weapons and the technology to manufacture them among the threshold countries; (c) the possible dangers to international security due to the failure of economic and political reform and the change in Russia; (d) the final threat to the US comes from the economic threat to America's future well-being which is the core of the "American Dream" and the basis of its social and political stability.

Secondly, the lessons of the Gulf War have had a definitive effect on America's post-Cold War military and defence strategy. In fact, one can see many of the conclusions reached by US experts in the congressional report, "Defence for a New Era: Lessons of the Persian Gulf War". A few examples in the context might be cited :

(a) The critical role of the air campaign in destroying the Iraqi nuclear and military infrastructure had led these experts to emphasise aviation technologies in both the Army and Navy budgets.

(b) The lesson that the use of high technology was a key reason for the high level performance of air and ground forces as well as minimising casualties gets reflected in emphasis on technological upgradation in all sectors of the military force structure. In this respect the Gulf War exposed also the tremendous lacunae in communications among the various sectors of the force structure which led to many mistakes in the air and land campaign.

(c) Militarily one lesson got clearly crystallised from the Gulf War, i.e. all future war preparations must be based on a single chain of command with a clear-cut distinction between the military and civilian roles of the theatre Commander-in-Chief.[5]

It should also be recapitulated that before 1968, the international community always clubbed chemical and biological weapons together. Any effort to deal with one variety had to take care of the other too. When negotiations for the elimination of both varieties of weapons began, the biological weapons were militarily almost redundant, while chemical weapons were much in use.

The United States of America had extensively deployed and applied chemical weapons in the killing fields of Vietnam. By 1972, the conclusion of a Biological Weapons Convention became a reality but any such thing for chemical weapons would not find consensus in the community of nations. The attempt towards the CWC certainly got independence and autonomy after the successful conclusion of the BWC. Since then, all problems, issues and negotiations related to chemical weapons were discussed and dealt with separately.

This explains why Washington has gone out of its way to threaten Iraq on the question of its stockpile of biological weapons.

Secondly, the anxiety and indignation of the US over nuclear tests by India and Pakistan too underlines how it would not allow other nations to acquire nuclear weapon capability.

There is something more to it than meets the eye. Notwithstanding the disintegration of the Soviet Union and "open market economy policies" of Russia, down deep the American policymakers have a lurking fear that Russia may re-emerge as a potential threat to the United States. Though the Cold War has ended, a technological upgradation of the defence forces of the US continues to be its top priority. This is the essence of the new strategic doctrine.

Seen in this context, it is relevant to underline that South Asia in the general American perception has become the region that is most likely to slip into accidental nuclear war in the post-Cold War years. This perception has become willy-nilly an article of faith among US officials, academics, and commentators. Some of them claim that India and Pakistan were alleged to be on the brink of what could have been a nuclear war in 1990.

In Washington's assessment the Indian subcontinent is one of Asia's "most dangerous flashpoint." This view is echoed by American scholars working on South Asian proliferation. Mitchell Reiss, for example, refers to the possibility of an outbreak of hostilities between India and Pakistan in 1987 and 1990, adding, "the risk of inadvertent or accidental nuclear war is now a fixture on the South Asian landscape."

This fear has been voiced through the US intelligence community as well. On February 24, 1993, testifying before the US Senate, the Central Intelligence Agency (CIA) Director James Woolsey cautioned: The arms race between India and Pakistan poses perhaps the most probable prospect for future use of weapons of mass destruction including nuclear weapons. Acknowledging this perception, seasoned US arms control experts noted in a professional journal: It has become commonplace to think of the Indian subcontinent as the most likely region where a war could escalate to a nuclear exchange.[6]

However, there are many contradictions in the account of the 1990 crisis. From the Indian perspective, for example, it appears that there was little or no awareness of the magnitude or nature of the danger that cast an ominious shadow over the subcontinent. There is also the curious dimension that the May 1990 crisis took almost three years to come into the public domain — this despite the fact that it was a commendable example of US preventive diplomacy at its most effective.[7]

In the final analysis, the nature of the May 1990 crisis still remains shrouded in a kind of subjective reality. Only the perspective and the perception change according to the location and nationality of the narrator. However, some facts and inferences that follow are irrefutable. These include: (1) Pakistan stepped up its covert LIC/State-sponsored terrorism against India from 1989 onwards, peaking in early 1990; (2) there was an input available to the United States (maybe through NSA intercept) that compelled the White House to invoke the Pressler Amendment in 1990, thereby acknowledging Pakistan's nuclear weapons capabilities; (3) in May 1990 itself there was evidence of certain activities by Pakistan that were suggestive of preparation for a nuclear weapon delivery.

The inferences that follow are: (1) Pakistan was emboldened by its nascent clandestine nuclear weapon perch to heighten its terrorist activities against India; (2) the United States which was prepared to turn a blind eye to Pakistan's nuclear weapon programme due to Cold War compulsions, may have inadvertently nurtured a clandestine nuclear weapon power over which it lost control; (3) Pakistan was treading a dangerous divide if it was indeed playing some kind of a nuclear charade either with the United States or India—or may be both.

The events of May 1990 have served to focus attention on one of the most muddied nuclear narrative known. US security interests in the Cold War and the subsequent China policy have resulted in a mixed bag of nuclear proliferation initiatives. Many myths have been created and nurtured in the South Asian context and consequently much of the analyses and debate are premised on the false analogies that Nietzsche had warned of. May 1990 needs to be revisited with greater candour by the nations involved to address the many unresolved issues of a crisis whose essential elements—clandestine nuclear weapons and the linkage with low-intensity conflict—directly affect their respective core security interests and, by extension, the stability of a turbulent post-Cold War Asia.[8]

Whatever may be the objective basis of this American assessment, the question arises why and how Pakistan was encouraged and promoted to acquire nuclear weapon capability?

Cold facts speak for themselves and need no comment.

Pakistan's Nuclear Weapons Capability

After the US-Pak military pact of 1955, slowly and steadily this neighbouring country of India came to occupy a strategic position in the US military doctrine. Thus both overtly and covertly Pakistan was encouraged to attain nuclear weapons capability. This conclusion is confirmed by the following facts :

1. Pakistan had begun the construction of a pilot plant at Sihala which went in operation in 1979; (2) the Kahuta nuclear facility was under construction at that stage; (3) in February 1977, weeks after Jimmy Carter entered the White House, one Princeton University student John Philips, was contacted to secure from him a copy of his plan to produce an atomic bomb; (4) in July 1977 *Nucleonics Week*, a US magazine claimed to have known that the private company Saint Gobian Techniques Nouveless had transferred about 95 per cent of solvent extraction know-how to Pakistan; (5) an agreement with the West German missile-making firm ORTAG was signed under which Pakistan got a large batch of intermediate-range missiles; (6) the Carter Administration in 1979 offered Pakistan economic and military aid of increased levels, particularly after the intervention of the Soviet Union in Afghanistan; (7) during the Reagan Administration in the 1976, the Symington Amendment which barred US aid to non-nuclear weapon countries importing uranium was

suspended and Islamabad was given aid of US dollars 3 billion for the next six years. One can go on giving facts to make out that it was Washington that sometimes overtly and sometimes covertly enabled Pakistan to become a nuclear weapons state and subsequently, China too played an important role in this regard.

In the post-Cold War period, there was no change in the American perception of Pakistan's role in this region. To give an example, when Pakistani Prime Minister Benazir Bhutto visited the USA (April 5-13, 1995), this became clear. In fact this visit had far-reaching consequences for India, particularly in such areas as nuclear proliferation and the acrimonious Kashmir issue. This was predicated not so much on the skill of the Pakistani Prime Minister in persuading her hosts but *in the convergence of apparent US intent to better India to a sub-continental matrix with a congenital Pakistani aspiration to seek perennial parity with its larger neighbour*.

The commitment by the US President that he would not abandon Pakistan and conferring of a strategic dimension to the US-Pak relationship in the post-Cold War years, acceptance by the US President of the Pakistani interpretation that Kashmir is at the core of the acrimonious Indo-Pak relationship, and the endorsement of the Pakistani position that the Pressler Amendment discriminates against Islamabad and a US resolve to work towards a regional nuclear solution that perceives India's nuclear dynamics only in an Indo-Pak context were put into place.

Pakistan is "a nation that aims to combine the best of the traditions of Islam with modern democratic ideals", stated President Clinton, "America is proud to claim Pakistan among her closest friends". Subsequently, Clinton in the course of his statements elaborated that Pakistan has been a good partner, and more importantly has stood for democracy, opportunity and moderation..."the future of the entire part of the world where Pakistan is depends in some large measure on Pakistan's success."[9]

Thus in the estimate of President Clinton "Pakistan is the closest friend" of the United States and the future of the Indian subcontinent "depends on Pakistan's success".

This is in contrast to the image/perception India evokes in some of Washington's highest government circles. For even while working in tandem with the USA on certain issues, New Delhi, at the best of times, evokes disquiet in the US Administration, the liberal, secular, democratic tag notwithstanding. Pakistan, on the other hand, even when indicted of the most severe excesses such as clandestine nuclear programmes, ethnic violence and terrorist acts is treated with indulgent benevolence.

Commenting on this visit, the *Washington Times*, a small newspaper that allegedly reflects US Administration views, was critical of Clinton's inability to lift the Pressler strictures unilaterally and noted editorially: The US is committing the error of rewarding our enemies and punishing our friends...nuclear proliferation is never a subject to be lightly addressed, but there is no reason to think that a nuclear capable Pakistan would be an international threat.

This interpretation was unambiguously endorsed by President Clinton, who in his overview of the turbulence that envelops the subcontinent noted: "Obviously, if the issue of Kashmir were resolved, a lot of these issues we have been discussing here today would resolve themselves. At least I believe that to be the case." Reiterating the familiar US position that Washington would play a role in Kashmir only if both parties are willing to have us play a leading role, the US President made a veiled reference to the question of elections in Kashmir the nuances of which merit attention. The Indians are now talking about elections (in Kashmir). It will be interesting to see who is eligible to vote, what the conditions of the elections are, whether it really is a free referendum of the people's will there.[11]

Thus till mid-90s, American perception about Pakistan was that : (1) it is the closest friend of the United States; (2) the future of the Indian sub-continent depends in some large measure on Pakistan; (3) a nuclear capable Pakistan would not be an international threat.

The same trend was reflected till the end of 1997 when Assistant Secretary of State for South Asia Karl Inderfurth said on 24 October 1997, that "the US strongly values its relationship with the Pakistani military and does not believe a powerful defence establishment in Islamabad undermines the civilian government of Prime Minister Nawaz Sharif."[12]

This assessment of the United States stands as a complete contrast to the new trends which began to unfold themselves since 1996, though this process began in the early 1990s. A wind of change began to blow over the Indian sub-continent. A series of steps were taken to normalise relations between India and Pakistan both at the official and non-official levels, particularly under the leadership of former Prime Minister I.K. Gujral.

To scuttle this development various levers were used. The most important was the moves of the Pentagon to build relations with the military elite of Pakistan.

This raises certain basic questions. Was the United States not trying to stall the process of normalisation of relations between India and Pakistan? Is this not a new version of policy of "divide and rule"? Are India and Pakistan not being pushed towards a confrontation as Iraq and Iran were before the Gulf War?

These are relevant questions. No one can give a ready-made answer to them because social science cannot be equated with astrology. However, it will be relevant here to recapitulate India's stand on weapons of mass destruction, including the nuclear weapons. We have to examine this question at a time when apprehension relating to the international security environment has been increased, rather than, as had been optimistically expected some years ago, diminished.

The NPT has been indefinitely extended. This single act resulted in the legitimisation, for the foreseeable future and beyond, of the possession of nuclear weapons by a few States and their possible use as a currency of power. This is not just India's view. That winding up of nuclear weapons is not yet part of the global agenda has also been demonstrated and emphasised to the world by subsequent events. Nuclear weapons states continue to spend hundreds of millions of dollars on their arsenals and plan on new facilities for continuing weapons-related research and development.

India's Stand : Global Nuclear Disarmament

India is justified in its scepticism as this undertaking was followed by reassertions by some of these countries citing reasons of their security, of their continuing need not only to possess these weapons but to ensure their reliability for use. Other developments, including announcements of "sub-critical" tests for the refinement of the nuclear weapons, and proposals for political discussions on the future role of nuclear weapons to ensure the security of some nuclear weapons states and their allies, and the inconsistency of these developments with the avowed goal of nuclear disarmament, have been noted by India with growing unease.

India is vitally interested in the progress of this process and would encourage its widening and deepening, since even after the planned reductions, huge stockpiles of weapons will remain. These existing weapons continue to pose a threat and it is on this that Indian attention is focused today.

Clearly, such a perpetually discriminatory environment will be perceived as unstable, provoking countries to unilateralism rather than collective security. Given the possibility of treating the perpetuation of the NPT as providing an indefinite licence to possess nuclear weapons it becomes even more imperative to have a legally binding commitment to eliminate these weapons in a specific time-frame.

Global nuclear disarmament has been a major objective of India's foreign policy since Independence. India is also conscious that disarmament cannot be achieved while proliferation continues. However, non-proliferation cannot be an end in itself and loses moral credibility unless it is unambiguously linked to disarmament. India has demonstrated its commitment to non-proliferation by voluntarily and unilaterally exercising the most rigorous control on its peaceful nuclear programme. Possession of nuclear weapons by any country constitutes a wider threat and this is not only a matter of principle but of the safety and security of all nations and all peoples.

CTBT: A First Step towards Complete Nuclear Disarmament

India joined the other members of G-21 in the Conference of Disarmament (CD) of an ad hoc Committee on Nuclear Disarmament to start negotiations on a phased programme with the eventual aim of eliminating all nuclear weapons within a time-bound framework.

Therefore, India is deeply disturbed that some States that possess nuclear weapons are unwilling to start addressing the security concerns of other States. That concerns on this issue are widely shared is evident from the clear messages received not only from the UN General Assembly but from Heads of States and Governments of the majority of the world community in Cartagena in 1995.

It is in this context that India envisions the future negotiations on a Comprehensive Test Ban Treaty (CTBT). To have a multilaterally negotiated CTBT was India's proposal four decades ago. Even at that time, we stated clearly that the CTBT was only a first step towards complete nuclear disarmament. If implemented then, the number of States with nuclear weapons and the number, types and the range of weapons in the possession of those that have then would have been very much less and, in India's opinion, nuclear disarmament would by now have been in our grasp. During these four decades the nuclear weapon

States have undertaken extensive testing programmes. This only makes it important that, as we take this step for a CTBT, we ensure that it is a step on the road to nuclear disarmament rather than into a cul-de-sac.

In India's view the CTBT must be an integral step in the process of nuclear disarmament. Developing new warheads or refining existing ones after the CTBT is in the place, using innovative technologies, would be as contrary to the spirit of the CTBT as the NPT is to the spirit of non-proliferation.

India is committed to working towards a CTBT that will promote the universally enunciated goal of total nuclear disarmament and thereby, the lasting and legitimate security interests of all countries in a nuclear weapon-free world including our own.

The treaty should be securely anchored in the global disarmament context and be linked through treaty language to the elimination of all nuclear weapons in a time-bound framework. India, therefore, intends to make concrete textual proposals in this regard at an appropriate stage so that the CTBT does not become just another flawed instrument aimed at curbing horizontal proliferation but a genuine disarmament step which terminates, for all States, without discrimination, the qualitative improvement and development of nuclear weapon systems. If the CTBT were to enter into force without a credible commitment to the elimination of nuclear weapons we would have lost yet another opportunity to work determinedly towards achieving a nuclear weapon-free world.

Another crucial issue relates to the scope of CTBT to ban all kinds of nuclear weapons testing. As the CTBT drove testing clandestine, we do not wish the CTBT to drive testing into the laboratories by those who have the resources to do so. We must ensure that the CTBT leaves no loophole for activity, either explosive based or non-explosive based, aimed at the continued development and refinement of nuclear weapons.

Consequently, this political intent needs to be reflected in the CTBT, clearly defining our objective—a treaty which will bring an end to all nuclear weapons development, not constrained by artificial limits of verification. The situation would be untenable where, even with a CTBT in place, development, refinement and production of new nuclear weapons continue. The CTBT, to be credible and meaningful, must be truly comprehensive and part of a genuine disarmament process.[12]

Notwithstanding the nuclear tests by India on May 11 and 13, 1998 and its unilateral announcement of moratorium of further nuclear tests, the basic features of its policy on nuclear weapons is as valid as before.

It was Jawaharlal Nehru who conceptualized this policy and brought into focus that "Great Powers" should not be allowed the status of "lord states". He said: "We are prepared in this, as in any other matter, even to limit, in common with other countries, our independence of action for the common good of the world. We are prepared to do that, provided we are assured that it is for the common good of the world and not exercised in a partial way and not dominated over by certain countries, however good their motives".[13]

The crux of the matter is that liquidation of weapons of mass destruction—nuclear, biological and chemical—has become a key link for the survival of humanity. This is precisely what has been attempted in this study, though we have dealt with biological and chemical weapons in greater details.

REFERENCES

1. John A. Vasquesz, : Keynote address to the Conference on New World Order/ New International Relations, Victoria University, Wellington New Zealand, December 8-9, 1994.
2. Patrick M. Regan; Department of Political Science, University of Canterbury Christchurch, New Zealand. The Party Intervention in Intra-State Conflicts, November, 1994.
3. Ralph Pettman; Professor of International Relations, Department of Politics, Victoria University of Wellington. The Paper presented at the New World Order/New International Relations, New Zealand Conference, Victoria University of Wellington, December 1994.
4. Deepankar Banerjee, Strategic Analysis, November 1995, pp. 1009-10.
5. Les Aspin and Dickinson, Defence for a New Era : Lessons of the Persian Gulf War (Washington, Brassey's 1992), pp. xx-xxii.
6. Strategic Digest, May 1998, Number 5, Vol. XXVII, pp. 729-30.
7. *Ibid.*, p. 730.
8. *Ibid.*, p. 739.
9. Strategic Analysis: July 1995, Vol. XVIII, No. 4, C. Uday Bhaskar, pp. 462-63.
10. *Ibid.*, pp. 463-64.
11. The Hindustan Times, 25/10/1997.
12. Arundhati Ghose,: Courtesy: Permanent Mission of India to United Nations Office, Geneva. : Strategic Digest : March 1996, Vol. XXVI, No. 3, pp. 303-5.
13. Jawaharlal Nehru's Speeches, Volume 33; 1953-57, Control of Nuclear Energy p. 257.

1

Weapons of Mass Destruction and Human Suffering

The woods are lovely, dark and deep,
But I have promises to keep,
And miles to go before I sleep,
And miles to go before I sleep.

These lines of Robert Frost, which Jawaharlal Nehru had copied and kept on his table till his death on 27th May, 1964, are relevant today, both literally and metaphorically, even after 34 years of his demise. Science and technology were to be employed, in Nehru's view, immediately and on a massive scale for the purpose of the industrialization of India. Britain's exploitation of India as an agricultural dependency being to him one of the worst aspects of imperialism, Nehru moved away from Gandhi's aversion to industrialization and was convinced that its promotion at all levels was of primary importance. As he said to Gandhi in 1940, if you sit on your large-scale industries, then other countries will sit on you. There was to him no hope of India coming into her own and consolidating her independence without industrialization. Few now dispute that this was the right policy. In an economy of the size of India's with a very large market, abundant natural resources of every kind and vast reserves of skilled and unskilled manpower, a strong and diversified base of capital goods is a historical necessity, indispensable for self-reliance, defence, technology for investment in agriculture, adequate production of consumer goods and development in other sectors. The advance attained, during Nehru's period, in the metallurgical, mechanical, chemical, power and transport sectors has provided India with the broad foundation of a modern economy.

It was this vision of Jawaharlal Nehru and to translate this dream into a reality he devoted his entire life. But this was only one dimension of his vision about India. He perhaps was one of the first leaders in the world who raised his voice against the arms race, elimination of all weapons of mass destruction—nuclear, chemical and biological.

Fifty-three years have passed since the cities of Hiroshima and Nagasaki in Japan were destroyed by the most dangerous weapons ever developed and used by mankind—the atom bomb. The horrors experienced more than five decades ago, however, are not merely matter of past historical interest. The atomic bombs of 1945 may have been small weapons compared to nuclear, chemical and biological weapons possessed by some nations by the standards of today's stockpile of weapons of mass destruction, but they unleashed the same multiple impact of heat, blast and radiation that characterise all weapons of mass destruction.

The instantaneous devastation suffered by Hiroshima and Nagasaki extended over unprecedentedly wide areas. Damages were so extensive that even today the full story is unclear. And the damaging effects have also extended over the years: many questions of radiation after-effects remain unsolved, and survivors still suffer anxieties about their physical and mental health.

The two cities' citizens went through experiences never known before, and thus they understood, unmistakably, that such tragedies must never be repeated on this planet. To that end they have, from that day to this, consistently appealed for the total abolition of nuclear arms and for the realization of true and permanent world peace.

Nuclear War and Future of our Planet

Today a nuclear war could destroy all living things on this earth. This warning, coming from scientists who have transcended their specific disciplines and nationalities, makes it clear that nuclear weapons are a kind of absolute evil. They must not be used for any reason, indeed even their possession cannot be condoned. As the agonies of Hiroshima and Nagasaki clearly foretell the sinister consequences of nuclear war, the developments of nuclear, chemical and biological weapons over the past fifty years make their abolition an inescapable conclusion today.

For a twenty-first century in which people can live in peace and without fear of total annihilation, the eradication of all weapons of mass destruction must be undertaken as the most essential requirement of human existence. For this purpose, it is crucial that the realities of what happened at Hiroshima and Nagasaki and later in Vietnam and in the Gulf region be widely and properly understood.

To preserve the Hiroshima-Nagasaki experience and to convey to peoples everywhere it is of first importance to have a complete and accurate record of the atom-bomb experiences of the two cities. It was this understanding that gave birth, through the devoted labours of editors Soichi, Seji Imahori, and Kanesaburo Gushima, to the comprehensive compilation *Hiroshima-Nagasaki no Genbaku Saigai* (A-bomb Damages of Hiroshima and Nagasaki) in 1979.

Today's nuclear arsenals have swollen to magnitudes of destructive power and global scope that utterly dwarf the first three atomic explosions of 1945, the initial test at Alamogordo, New Mexico, and the primitive bombs used at Hiroshima and Nagasaki. Countries now possessing nuclear arms include the United States, the Soviet Union— now Russia, Britain, France and China—and other nations reportedly are developing their own nuclear weapons. The United States and the Soviet Union, now Russia, of course, are the unmatched nuclear superpowers, with weapons systems incomparably greater and more sophisticated than all others combined.

In the mid-80s the United States had some 9,500 nuclear warheads for use on strategic weapons; the Soviet Union, about 8,400. These represented an overall destructive capability comparable to 3,400 megatons of conventional (TNT) explosives for the United States and 4,100 megatons for the Soviet Union. For tactical weapons, estimated warhead counts are 20,000 (USA) and 15,000 (USSR). Even tactical warheads have many times the destructive force of a Hiroshima-type bomb; the combined American-Soviet holdings were roughly equivalent to 4,500 megatons of TNT. The two superpowers thus held in the mid-80s in readiness an aggregate strategic-tactical destructive capability of 12,000 megatons. This is the equivalent force of one million Hiroshima-type bombs.

The nuclear peril, however, consists not only in vastly expanded destructive power but also in increasingly diverse and sophisticated delivery systems–intercontinental ballistic missiles (ICBMs), submarine-launched ballistic missiles (SLBMs), multiple individually targeted re-entry vehicles (MIRVs), intermediate-range missiles (SS-20, Pershing II), cruise missiles, and the neutron bomb, along with long-range super bombers, nuclear-powered submarines and military satellites. These systems represent striking technological advances in launching, targetting, and delivery capabilities. They also bring the world much closer to the very real and grim possibility of all–out nuclear warfare that could literally destroy the human race and its planetary home. The situation has become more complex with the development and use of chemical and biological weapons. We will come to this aspect later on in this study.

Tragedies of Hiroshima and Nagasaki

Compared with the extinction prospects of nuclear war today, the A-bomb damages suffered by Hiroshima and Nagasaki fifty-three years ago seem small indeed. Yet those damages, even if limited by today's standards, provide the only concrete experiential basis for assessing what really happens to people and societies subjected to nuclear attack. The Hiroshima-Nagasaki experience, therefore, is the starting-point for projecting and from this we see the absolute necessity for preventing the irreversible devastation that would result from use of current nuclear weapons. Nuclear winter is a frightening prospect; but how many people would actually survive, and in what wretched conditions, to experience it? Options for battlefield and war-theatre use of nuclear weapons are increasing, as is the dangerous likelihood of such use. But the question as to whether localized or limited employment of nuclear weapons can be tolerated has already been answered in the 1945 tragedies of Hiroshima and Nagasaki. The cries of No more Hiroshimas and No more Nagasakis arise from the innermost depths of the survivors of the holocaust from the two cities' citizens who tasted the bitter ashes of the world's first atomic hellfires. From their seared spirits comes the uncompromising warning that nuclear war—completely eclipsing the Hiroshima-Nagasaki horrors—must never be unleashed on the world, anywhere, for any reason.

But this tragic story will remain incomplete if we do not take into account the use of chemical, biological and toxic weapons used later on in Vietnam and in the Gulf region. But before we analyse it let us recapitulate the impact of atomic bomb on the people of Hiroshima and Nagasaki and how generation after generation of the Japanese people are suffering even today.

In the early morning of 6th August, 1945, an American army observation plane from the Tinian air base invaded the skies of Hiroshima at an altitude of 10,000 metres. The exact time when the air-raid alert was sounded by the Hiroshima Chugoku Regional Headquarters was 7:09 a.m.

Minutes later, however, the Enola Gay, conveyer of the atomic bomb, accompanied by two weather observation planes invaded the skies of Hiroshima from the north–east. The Enola Gay then released the atomic bomb at 8:15:27 a.m. from an altitude of 9,000 metres—the atomic bomb exploded 43 seconds later.

9th August, 1945. It was a quiet summer day in Nagasaki. A dense morning mist started to clear gradually from 7 a.m. At 11 a.m. the temperature was 28.8°C. Although air-raid alerts and alarms were sounded several times on this day, the people in this city returned to work when the alarms were turned off.

The B-29 Bock's Car, conveyer of the atomic bomb, left the Tinian air base in the early morning and was joined by a weather observation plane in the skies over Yakushima. At 9:50 a.m. they reached the skies of Kokura, their first target. Since the skies of Kokura were covered by heavy clouds and visibility was poor, seven minutes later they headed for Nagasaki, their second target. The skies of Nagasaki were also covered by clouds, but a gap appeared for an instant between the clouds. Down below was seen the Mitsubishi Heavy Industries Nagasaki Arsenal.

The atomic bomb was released at 11:02 a.m. The height of the burst point was about 503 metres, and ground zero is assumed to have been located at coordinated 1293.624 ± 0.007 (longitude 129° 51′56′4E) ×1065.936 ± 0.008 (latitude 32° 46′12′6N). This is about 90 metres east-southeast of the main intersection of Matsuyama township, the site where the Peace Memorial Statue stands in today's Heiwa-koean (Peace Park).

This in brief, was the beginning of human tragedy that too by using scientific achievements. Anyone who visits Hiroshima and stands before the peace memorial statue and lays a wreath on the memorial of unsung and unwept victims of the atomic bomb cannot but spiritually develop a sense of guilt. This was precisely the experience of this writer on three occasions, the last being by the end of 1986. This sense of guilt comes to you because even after more than five decades, the weapons of mass destruction continue to be paraded with pride and in some cases used as what is called instrument of 'political deterrence'. Voices for building a nuclear weapon-free and non-violent world are still feeble and weak and consequently stifled by the powers-that-be.

Let us now examine how the Japanese people, the first victims of the atomic bomb, suffered after this tragedy.

Hiroshima's buildings were reduced to rubble and ashes by a combination of blast wave and heat radiation. The buildings were first demolished by blast force and then consumed by raging fires that left 13 square kilometres of scorched wasteland. The fires resulted from primary ignition by heat rays and from secondary ignition as structures collapsed. Erupting almost simultaneously in many places about thirty minutes after the bombing, the fires merged into a huge conflagration. Air in the flaming area became heated, causing a rapid rush of air upward with cooler air flowing in from all directions. This phenomenon is called a firestorm. Hiroshima's conflagaration-produced firestorm reached a velocity of 18 metres per second two or three hours later. Moreover, from 11 a.m. to 3 p.m. a violent whirlwind blew locally from the centre towards the northern part of the city. These fierce winds expanded the fires; and within a 2-kilometre radius of ground zero, everything flammable was completely reduced to ashes. Within 3 kilometres, 90 per cent of the buildings were completely demolished and burnt. Even within a 4-kilometre radius, there was massive destruction; 68 per cent of all buildings were completely demolished and burnt with 34 per cent half-demolished and half-burnt. Only 6,180 structures, 8 per cent in this larger area remained usable.

Fires broke out in many places beyond the 2 kilometres distance from ground zero, though mostly from secondary ignition as buildings collapsed. But even at a 3-kilometre distance, primary ignition by the bomb's heat rays set aflame straw roofs, timber, hillside forests, and other naturally inflammable materials.

Though this shows how widespread was the impact of this 'mini' atom bomb what needs to be underlined is the human sufferings that resulted. Though it is difficult to determine the exact number of the people killed by this atom bomb, the various surveys show that 57 per cent to 61 per cent of Hiroshima's population lived within 2 kilometres and 81 per cent to 87 per cent within 3 kilometres of the place where this bomb exploded. Hiroshima's population on the bombing date is estimated to be 2,80,000 to 2,90,000. In addition to this there were another 43,000 army personnel in Hiroshima on that day. This means that more than 3.40 lakh people were in Hiroshima on the day of bombing.

According to the various estimates made by Hiroshima authorities immediately after this atomic bomb was exploded, at least 80,000 people were killed soon after the blast. However, though this figure shows that every 3rd person in Hiroshima died, this does not reflect accurately the devastation caused by this blast. A large number of people died of the injuries caused by this blast and there were many more who died because of serious harm to their bodies caused by radiation. However, the subsequent survey shows that this death toll was higher than was estimated soon after explosion of the bomb. But this alone does not reflect the havoc caused by this bomb.

This atomic bomb demolished Hiroshima and left the city areas engulfed in veritable hellfire. What is more distressing than this is that besides the immediate death of nearly one lakh persons in Hiroshima, more than 3 lakh persons in and around Hiroshima received serious injuries and were treated in various hospitals. This gives only a partial estimate of the devastation caused by this bomb in terms of death and serious injuries. There is something more to it which every peace-loving person should bear in mind. This relates to impact of radiation on the people, their children and grandchildren both in Hiroshima and Nagasaki.

The radiation released by the air-burst of an atomic bomb can be divided into two categories: initial radiation, emitted within one minute of the explosion; and residual radiation, confirmed later in the area exposed to the atomic bomb. An enormous amount of radiation was released by the atomic bomb, a crucial difference from a conventional bomb. This led to the great degree and extent of sufferings of the many people exposed to the atomic bomb.

The initial radiation of an atomic bomb consists of alpha particles, beta particles, gamma rays, and neutrons. Alpha rays are released from uranium and plutonium, which have escaped fission, and beta rays from fission products. Because of the short ranges in air of alpha and beta particles, these rays failed to reach ground level. Consequently gamma rays and neutrons of initial radiation were the ones that had the key effects on the human beings, animals, and plants. The energy of these rays was about 3 per cent of the total energy emitted by the explosion.

Gamma rays : Gamma rays are produced during nuclear fission of uranium or plutonium when neutrons released by fission are absorbed by surrounding atomic nuclei, and form a variety of products of nuclear fission. The main gamma rays reaching the ground are the products of nuclear fission.

Neutrons : Neutrons are one of the particles comprising the atomic nuclei. Though they are electrically neutral elementary particles, the energy of neutrons released on Hiroshima and Nagasaki was assumed to be proportional to the square of velocity. Neutrons are classified as fast and slow. For example, the velocity of a 1 mega-electronvolt fast neutron is 1.4 × 10 metres per second but a thermal neutron of a 0.025 electronvolt is a slow neutron with a velocity of 2.2 × 10 metres per second. Most of the neutrons released during nuclear fission are fast neutrons. Though some of these neutrons are delayed by elastic collisions with the nuclei penetrating the bomb materials and cause a chain reaction of nuclear fission, most neutrons are emitted into the air. Neutrons scattered in the air are slowed down by collisions with the nuclei of nitrogen and oxygen, but those not absorbed reach the ground almost instantaneously.

To know the dose and nature of the radiation received at ground level at the time of explosion of the atomic bombs in Hiroshima and Nagasaki is extremely important and basically essential in understanding what an atomic bomb can do to human beings. Estimation of radiation dose was commenced soon after the explosion. Among samples collected on 13th and 14th August in Hiroshima, abnormally strong beta particles were detected in the bones of a horse, and radioactivity from neutrons. Furthermore, inducted radioactivity (Phosphorus 32; half-life 14.3 days) was detected in human bones on 16th August. The bones of victims were collected until early September. Measurements of radioactivity revealed the concentration of fast neutrons at ground zero in Hiroshima to be 1.2×10^{12} neutrons per square cm. and slow neutrons to be 9×10^{12} neutrons per sq. cm. In Nagasaki the concentration of neutrons was estimated to be 8×10^{12} neutrons per sq. cm. from the measurements of radioactivity in bone on 23rd October near ground zero.

In-air dose: No definite value of the estimated in-air dose for a distance from ground zero has yet been obtained. Based on the experimental data in the United States after 1955, dosimetry studies for estimating the actual exposure dose of subjects have been carried out at the Oak Ridge National Laboratory and in 1957 the T57D (tentative 1957 dose) by distance was proposed for the first time by E.N. York. On the other hand, basic studies by Japanese scientists in the period 1958-60 led to the development of a radiochemical method by which the exposure dose of neutrons could be estimated. Iron material used for construction contains minute amounts of non-radioactive cobalt and when neutrons are absorbed radioactive cobalt 60 is produced. Estimation of initial gamma-ray dose by thermoluminescence was made on bricks and tiles collected at various distances from ground zero. Thermoluminescence is a weak light emitted by an oxide heated to a high temperature, in this case about 300 °C. Since the luminosity is proportional to the latent energy retained in the matter or substance by exposure to radiation, it is possible to estimate the initial gamma-ray exposure to each location. By applying these two methods, Hashizume and Maryama of the National Institute of Radiological Sciences (NIRS) succeeded in obtaining an in-air dose corresponding to the distance from the previously estimated values in Hiroshima and Nagasaki.

In 1966 the Oak Ridge National Laboratory, after having continued its study on radiation-dose estimation, reported the tentative 1965 dose (T65D). While the T57D curve proposed by York represents the estimated values obtained indirectly and based on the nature of the atomic bombs dropped on Hiroshima and Nagasaki, the T65D was reassessed by further adding the data obtained by the series of experiments carried out in Nevada. When comparing the in-air dose curves obtained by the estimated values of T57D, T65D, and NIRS, the T65D curve is lower than the T57D curve in Hiroshima, and the NIRS curve is within the estimated error limits of T65D curve. Since the estimated values of T65D and NIRS are quite similar, the T65D has been the most widely used in-air dose up to the present time.

When comparing the radiation dose by the distance from ground zero, T65D is characterized by the high dose of neutrons in Hiroshima and by the higher dose of gamma rays in Nagasaki. The dose of neutrons in Nagasaki was almost negligible, while about 20 per cent of the radiation dose received by the people in Hiroshima were neutrons. Since the injurious effects of neutrons are considered to be about ten times greater than those of gamma rays, the effects on human subjects may be said to have been caused by neutrons. This difference between the two cities was probably brought about by the differences in structure and content to of Little Boy and Fat Man, the code names of the two A-bombs dropped in Japan.

Fairly recently, the estimated values of radiation exposure dose in Hiroshima and Nagasaki have been revised by scientists at the Lawrence Livermore National Laboratory (LLNL) and the Oak Ridge National Laboratory (ORNL). Their results differ significantly from those of T65D. The establishment of a new estimated dose of radiation energy-spectra at the time of the atomic bomb explosions in Hiroshima and Nagasaki, which was not clear when T65D was estimated, led to the reassessment of atomic-bomb radiation dosimetry. To begin with the entire picture and details of the structure and components of Little Boy and Fat Man have not been revealed. The spectra of gamma rays and neutrons released by the Hiroshima type and Nagasaki-type atomic bombs were, however, made public for the first time by the Los Alamos National Laboratory (LANL) in 1976. With this new information on the spectra estimated dose, the LLNL and the ORNL group recalculated the in-air dose of gamma rays and neutrons, and the results were reported in 1981-82, respectively.

According to the new calculation, the in-air dose of gamma rays in Hiroshima was higher than the value of the T65D, while in Nagasaki it was lower. On the other hand, thc estimated neutron dose in both cities was lower than the new value obtained by the revised calculation. The relative estimated dose of neutrons in Hiroshima calculated by both laboratories was significantly lower than the value of T65D. In other words, they concluded that there was no neutron radiation of any statistical significance present at Hiroshima after the bombing. At present, no conclusions have been reached on the reassessment of radiation dosimetry. Since 1983, the Radiation Effects Research Foundation (RERF) in Hiroshima and Nagasaki has established a US-Japan joint workshop for reassessment of atomic bomb radiation dosimetry, and the final report of this joint workshop is expected to be issued in the near future.

The in-air dose of gamma rays and neutrons hitherto mentioned is the dose to which the subjects were exposed without shielding. Though this dose may serve as a scale for estimating exposure dose, the shielding effects of house, shelters, and buildings must also be considered.

The actual shielding conditions at the time of the explosion varied greatly. Studies on this problem have been carried out from 1952 by the Atomic Bomb Casualty Commission (ABCC) and at the Oak Ridge National Laboratory. The actual exposure dose received by each individual has been estimated by taking into account the Japanese style of structure, each person's position inside a house and his or her distance from the windows, and the shape of the structure and its location. When the actual shielding conditions were unclear, the mean penetration coefficient was used.

Even when the in-air dose of gamma rays and neutrons received by human subjects under various shielding conditions is obtained, the actual dose is that which acts on the skin surface. In studying radiation injury, one still needs to know the dose absorbed by various organs and tissues. According to the study made at the National Institute of Radiological Sciences, when one is exposed from one direction outdoors, the gamma rays and neutrons received by the centre of the body would diminish to about one-half and one-tenth, respectively, of those acting on the surface of the body.

By residual radiation is meant the radiation remaining in the exposed area for a definite period after the explosion. The sources of residual radiation are induced radioactivity and fallout.

When neutrons are absorbed by a substance, atomic nuclei destruction of some of the elements constituting the substance occurs and is followed by emission of radiation such as beta particles and gamma rays for a certain period of time.

When neutrons emitted by the explosion of the atom bombs in Hiroshima and Nagasaki reached ground level, absorption of neutrons by substances on and in soil led to induced radioactivity. On 10th and 11th August in Hiroshima, radioactivity was detected in soil collected from areas several hundred metres from ground zero, while on 13th August in Nagasaki it was also found in soil near to ground zero. The slow neutrons were the main source of induced radioactivity of substances, and the intensity of induced radioactivity was proportional to the energy of neutrons and the total number of neutrons.

The duration of radiation emission differs according to the kind of radioisotope. Among the various radioisotopes detected in the bombed area, aluminium 28, manganese 56 and sodium 24 have a short half-life and disappeared almost completely after 100 hours or more after the explosion. On the other hand, scandium 46, cobalt 60 and cesium 134 have a long half-life though minute in quantity. In order to determine their effects on the human body, it is necessary to estimate the exposure dose of gamma rays emitted by these radioisotopes. The dose rate of gamma rays of induced radioactivity was estimated 1 metre above ground immediately after the explosion at ground zero in Hiroshima. The dose decreases with distance from ground zero. Since the radioisotopes lose their radioactivity in accordance with their half-life, the dose rate of gamma rays falls with time.

The total gamma ray dose from induced radioactivity up to 100 hours after the explosion 1 meter above ground at ground zero in Hiroshima verged at about 100 rads. This value was about 20 rads at a distance of 500 metres and about 1 rad at 1,000 metres. After 100 hours the gamma ray dose from induced radioactivity decreased rapidly.

The fallout of an atomic bomb is composed of nuclear fission products of uranium or plutonium isotopes that have escaped fission, and weapon residues activated by neutrons. These minute particles are blown high into the atmosphere and move with the wind. They descend gradually or come down concentrated on a specific area. Rain is considered to be one condition that prompts their downfall.

In Hiroshima a 1-3 metre per second wind was blowing from the south-east at the time of the explosion. Twenty to thirty minutes later a huge mushroom cloud formed by the explosion moved gradually towards the north-west. Heavy rain continued for more than an hour over an elliptical area, 19 by 11 kilometres, towards the north-west, including the destroyed area within 2 kilometres of ground zero. The rain was called black rain—a sticky and muddy rain, which contained the fallout. The air temperature fell rapidly in the midst of the heavy rainfall, and many people were shivering in mid-summer. The area where dusty ash fell extended several kilometres outside the rainy area, and this was also recorded in Shimane Prefecture at a distance of more than 50 km.

The cloud formed by the Nagasaki A-bomb was observed from the Onsendake Meteorological Station at Mount Unzen 45 km. east of ground zero. At about 11.40 a.m. the cumulonimbus cloud was observed and black smoke below the cloud were seen. The cloud bottom was estimated to be 1,200 to 1,300 metres high, and the cloud top 4,000 to 5,000 metres. At about 12.10 p.m. the cloud started to go out of shape towards the east-northeast. Thereafter the mushroom cloud moved towards the east and at 2 p.m. passed over the vicinity of Mount Unzen. The rain started to fall approximately 40 minutes after the explosion in the vicinity of Mount Konpira located about 2 kilometres east of ground zero. Considerable rainfall was also seen 20 minutes after the explosion in the Nishiyama district east of Mount Konpira. There were intermittent showers, admixed with ashes, until night. The rainfall in Nishiyama district was the black rain, and concentrated amounts of radioactive materials were assumed to have fallen here. A light rainfall was recorded between 1.50 p.m. and 2 p.m. at Mount Unzen.

Dust and ashes fell on the villages of Yagami, Toishi, Koga, Kikitsu, Tayu, and Enoura, and on Isahaya city located north-east of Nagasaki.

Right after the bombing, three radiosondes, each attached to a parachute, were dropped from a weather observation plane. These radiosondes were carried away towards the east and fell on Kamikochi, Hotogi, and Dake at 11.30 a.m., noon, and 1 p.m. respectively. These facts show that an east-northeast wind with a 3 metres per second velocity had probably been blowing at bombing time in Nagasaki.

About 200 different kinds of radioactive isotopes were produced by the explosion of the atomic bomb. Analyses of soil in the Nishiyama district revealed strontium 89, barium 140, praseodymium 144, zirconium 95, strontium 90, cesium 137 and cesium 144. Furthermore, plutonium 239 that had escaped fission was also detected. According to the actual gamma-ray dose rate at 1 metre above ground, a maximum 0.045 milliroentgen per hour was recorded in the area 3-4 kilometres to the west of ground zero in Hiroshima, while a maximum 1 milliroentgen per hour was recorded in the Nishiyama district of Nagasaki. These estimated values correspond to 4-44 rads 15 centimetres above ground in Hiroshima and 30-149 rads in the Nishiyama district of Nagasaki.

Since fallout is taken into the body by inhalation, and through contaminated food and drinking water, radiation effects on the body are seen in the form of internal radiation. Radioisotopes with a long half-life remain in the body for a long time. Measurement of radioactive substances active on humans between 1969 and 1971 revealed that the amount of cesium 137 in the residents of the Nishiyama district in Nagasaki was nearly twice that in other districts.

Injury to the human body by an atomic bomb is caused by a complex action of thermal rays, blast, and radioactive rays. The miserable and serious condition called atomic bomb injury or atomic bomb illness resulted from a catastrophe never before experienced by mankind. The numerous A-bomb casualties occurred almost simultaneously, within seconds after the explosion; and the thermal rays, blasts, and radioactive rays became attenuated with distance from the burst point. The injurious action was, however, weakened by shielding. The severity of atomic bomb injury was roughly in inverse proportion to the distance between the site of exposure and ground zero.

A 50 per cent death rate on the day of explosion is presumed in those exposed at 1.2 kilometres from ground zero, and in time an 80 per cent to 100 per cent death rate in those within this distance. Even among those escaping instant death or death on the same day of exposure, the mortality rate later became extremely high in those exposed at close proximity and in those sustaining severe injuries.

What is more disturbing is that even after 53 years of explosion of this atom bomb its effect on the health of the people, children and grandchildren of those who became victims of this blast are visible. These effects have come to light recently. In these areas it was found for instance that some people had developed cataract because of presence of radioactive elements in their genes.

Leukemia in the exposed was first found in 1945 at Nagasaki and in 1946 at Hiroshima. The incidence of leukemia among the exposed became higher in the following years, and reached its peak between 1950 and 1953. A few years later, there was an increased incidence of thyroid cancer, breast cancer, lung cancer, salivary gland cancer, and other cancers among people who had been exposed to the atomic bomb. The effects on the first filial and second filial generations of atomic bomb victims and other genetic effects are important subjects still being studied.

Genetic Effects

Since genetic effects on offspring following irradiation have been known to occur in experimental studies, there was great concern about possible genetic effects in the offspring of people exposed to the atomic bombs in Hiroshima and Nagasaki. Careful genetic surveys have been carried out over the years since then, focusing on spontaneous abortions and still-births due to lethal mutations, infantile deaths resulting from harmful effects during the foetal stage, increased frequency of congenital malformations in parents, change in sex ratio, mortality rate, and birth weight and height of children.

Furthermore, in order to see whether any changes in genes have occurred when not accompanied by apparent changes in shape of the body or of cells, biochemical genetic studies are being carried out on serum protein to detect any gene mutations.

Genetic surveys undertaken to date have yielded no positive evidence of a genetic hazard due to atomic bomb radiation. It is, however, possible that genetic effects do not show up so distinctly in human beings, since the interval between two successive generations is long, the abortion rate is high, and they have relatively few children. Since the difficulties accompanying genetic survey and study are in reality much greater than one may assume, it will take many more years of observation and study in order to understand the genetic effects of atomic bomb exposure. However, the fact that no decisive, harmful genetic effects of atomic bomb radiation have been observed to date among those exposed in Hiroshima and Nagasaki is at least a consolation as far as the atomic bomb casualties in both cities are concerned.

Many survivors, from the bombings to the present have had to endure a wide variety of hardships. One special concern has been the damages to body and mind. A-bomb injuries and illnesses have already been discussed in some detail; of these long-lasting effects stemmed from acute A-bomb diseases and especially light and severe radiation illness, anemia, damage to reproductive functions, and lowered resistance to infection. Retarded healing of burns and external wounds also caused considerable distress. The combination of inordinate psychological shock with various bodily injuries, moreover, produced diverse psychosomatic symptoms, general malaise, and anxiety about illness. These problems plagued many survivors for several years after the bombing, and in many cases for more than ten years.

Another common condition was nourashnia, or neurosis accompanied by generalised fatigue, languid hands and feet, and resting from work five or six times more often than healthy persons—after working one whole day they often took off two or three days. Patients suffering from whole-body fatigue found it difficult to rest, especially in summer time. Many experienced extreme loss of memory, emotional instability, gross impatience, inefficiency, and were easily frightened by ordinary but sudden sights and sounds. Such disorders plagued patients for varying periods of time.

As after-effects such as cataracts, leukemia, and a variety of cancers began occurring with rising frequency among A-bomb survivors, others naturally feared they too might fall victim to these diseases. Then, with the passing years ageing and geriatric diseases became causes for anxious concern. Radiation effects accelerated ageing and shortened lifespan, as demonstrated in animal experiments, have not been statistically established, in either frequency or degree, among the A-bomb survivor groups studied.

A number of problems, however, are indicated. According to observations made between 1958 and 1974 the incidences of brain hemorrhage and coronary heart diseases were found significantly high among women in Hiroshima who had been exposed to large doses of radiation. This tendency was most evident in women exposed at a young age. Epidemiological surveys on the relations among infection, inflammation, immunity, and exposure to the atomic explosion have revealed no effects of radiation. However, the morbidity rate of hepatitis was found to be high in those exposed to large doses of radiation; the function of lymphocytes, which play an important role in immunity, was altered in elderly persons receiving large doses of radiation; and an abnormal antibody reaction to influenza was found in those exposed in utero. At least some of the exposed people were affected by radiation and became ill as they grew older.

The fate of all survivors is to live with the stigma that the atomic bomb stamped permanent marks on their minds and bodies. Certainly history's most massive act of destruction imposed on them an abhorrent lifelong burden to live with and try to overcome—one that exceeds the limits of verbal expression.

The tragic story of Hiroshima and Nagasaki still stirs the emotions of the people of these two cities, the Japanese people in general and all the peace-loving people in the world who abhor the concept of using nuclear weapons, either to establish hegemony on the world or use it for what is called a political deterrence.

Famous Japanese poet Sankichi Toge in his short and moving poem has articulated the feelings of the first victims of the atomic bomb. This poem now is carved on his memorial monument.

Give back my father, give back my mother,
Give grandpa back, grandma back,
Give me my sons and daughters back.

Give me back myself,
Give back the human race.

As long as this life lasts, this life,
Give back peace
That will never end.

That is why Jawaharlal Nehru in his speech in the UN General Assembly, New York, on October 3, 1960 reminded the world that "the League of Nations appeared to be unconcerned and discussed all manner of subjects except the most vital subject of the day .... After many years of carnage, the war ended and a new age—the atomic age was ushered in by the terrible experience of Hiroshima and Nagasaki."

Nevertheless, anyone who knows Indian history will agree that it was Jawaharlal Nehru who laid the foundations for development of science and technology and nuclear technology for peaceful purposes. Amongst the inner circles of his advisors could be counted the leader of Indian science at the time—Dr. Homi Bhabha of Nuclear Science, Sir Shanti Swarup Bhatnagar, and his successor as Director General of the Council of Scientific and Industrial Research, Prof. M.S. Thacker and Dr. Daulat Singh Kothari, the first scientific advisor to the Ministry of Defence.

Nevertheless, his vision is as relevant today as when he was alive.

We have "miles to go" to build a nuclear weapon-free and a non-violent world.

Hiroshima and Nagasaki are still the living symbols of the aspirations of the people on our planet.

REFERENCES

1. *The Impact of the atomic-bomb*, Hiroshima and Nagasaki, 1945-84, pp. 1-3- 4, 6.
2. *The Impact of the atomic-bomb*, Hiroshima and Nagasaki, Iwanami Shoten.
3. Hiroshima Peace Science, Institute for Peace Science, Hiroshima University.
4. Papers presented at the Hiroshima Symposium: *50 Years of Nuclear Weapons*, September 17-18, 1996 (Hiroshima Perfectural Cultural Center).

[illegible]

[illegible]

REFERENCES

[illegible]

[illegible]

2

The Atomic Bomb: Collective Memory and Historians

Hideki Kan
Kyushu University (Japan)

According to the author, several studies have been noted how the American air doctrine transformed the wartime morality during the World War II. The American airpower doctrine accepted the principle that in modern total war, civilians and armed forces were inseparably linked in national war machines and that one way to break those machines was to smash civilian will. The concept of strategic bombing marked the break with tradition in which war had been primarily against combatants. The moral revolution caused by indiscriminate killings of civilians in city bombings was given up. American leaders, both political and military, were largely immune to the mass killing of civilians. It was this redefinition of morality that made Hiroshima and Nagasaki possible. The dropping of the A-bomb was a culmination of the concept of strategic bombing and the resultant transformation of wartime morality. The most important aspect of this new strategy was to produce the greatest psychological effect on Japan and to make the world, and the Soviet Union in particular, aware that America possessed this new power. This conclusion is as relevant today as it was fifty-three years ago.

The cancellation of the National Air and Space Museum's original Enola Gay exhibition in January, 1995 and the heated controversy preceding it clearly indicated that there still exists after fifty years' wide gap between Japanese and American perceptions of the A-bomb decision. The psychological and cognitive dissonance over the question has constituted a serious irritant in US-Japan relations. Japanese tend to feel that the A-bombs were unnecessary to end the war; they feel that the killing of more than 210,000 civilians, not combatants by the atomic destruction of the two cities cannot be justified even if one considers the wartime circumstances. They, therefore, would like to hear the Americans express "regret" or an "apology". On the other hand, many Americans feel even today just as President Truman did, that the bomb was regarded as "a military weapon" and never had any doubt that it should be used. Many Americans also accept Truman's explanation that the bomb was dropped to bring the war to an early end as well as to save half a million American lives. They also have strong emotions about the Japanese attack on Pearl Harbour and feel that the Japanese should apologize for the attack. Thus we are trapped in the habit of mutual recrimination (the "Pearl Harbour-Hiroshima Syndrome"). As a way to break out of this impasse, this article examines the nature of the debate and historical findings of the A-bomb decision in order to locate an area of the emerging scholarly consensus. To that end, we will review the literature on this topic along the following issues: (1) the motives and reasons leading to President Truman's decision to use the bomb, (2) the question of alternatives, (3) evaluation of justifications for the dropping of the bomb, (4) collective memory and the role of historians. The paper will suggest that new findings and their implications be incorporated into history textbooks at the secondary and college levels. By so doing historians can contribute to a better understanding of this monumental decision. Such an undertaking will hopefully help us break this vicious cycle of the "victim-victimizer syndrome" and narrow the gaps of collective memory between the two nations.

WHY WAS THE BOMB DROPPED?

As is well known, the controversy over the reasons for Truman's decision arose when revisionist historians' challenged "orthodox" interpretations. The 'orthodox historians' like Herbert Feis argued that the bomb was used to bring the war to a quick end as well as to save thousands of lives.[1] Professor Gar Alperovitz challenged this orthodoxy in his influential book, *Atomic Diplomacy,* first published in 1965. He emphasized the "Soviet factor" as central to the decision to use the atomic bomb. The following factors weigh heavily in his interpretation: the increasing intensity of Japanese peace feelers and US leaders' knowledge of the emperor's initiative, Washington's increasing awareness that Japan was militarily defeated and that dropping the bomb was unnecessary, the forthcoming impact of Soviet entry, the Japanese ruling elite's minimum surrender condition of retaining the emperor system. The fact that available alternatives to the bomb were rejected explains, according to Alperovitz, that the bomb was dropped to make the Russians more manageable in deteriorating Soviet-American relations.[2]

A third interpretation emerged during the 1970s. Professor Barton J. Bernstein argued that Truman and most of his advisors conceived the A-bomb as "a legitimate weapon" to be used against the enemy and that the combat use of it seemed "necessary and desirable" to end the war on American terms, avoid the dreaded invasion, punish the Japanese for Pearl Harbour and their mistreatment of POWs, fulfil bureaucratic needs, conform to the desire of the American people, and also to intimidate the Soviets. Though he admits that there was an anti-Soviet motive in Truman's decision, he significantly differs from Alperovitz: Bernstein contends that the prospect of intimidating the Soviets was "a kind of bonus", not "the dominant purpose for using the weapon."[3]

Feis, in his revised 1961 edition of his earlier book, came to admit that there was the "Soviet factor" in the decision, a revision necessitated by Alperovitz's work. Thus these three major interpretations admit that the "Soviet factor" was a consideration in Truman's decision to use the A-bomb. The significant point of disagreement is a difference in emphasis: the revisionist historians regard the "Soviet factor" as the primary reason for Truman's decision, while Bernstein's "bonus" thesis regards intimidating the Soviets as "a confirming and not the controlling reason". In this connection, I might add that Martin J. Sherwin basically agrees with Bernstein except that Sherwin considers the "Soviet factor" as more important than "a bonus".[4]

Bernstein's arguments and evidence produced to support his thesis are quite impressive. It is also possible to claim, as Bernstein does, that "the bomb would undoubtedly have been used even if the Soviet Union had not existed."

Unfortunately for Bernstein, however, the Soviet Union existed. The "Soviet factor" was not as negligible as he claims. In the summer of 1945 Truman and his top policy makers faced two urgent tasks: one was to end the war as quickly as possible without an invasion, and the other was how to deal with the Soviet Union in the postwar settlements derived from

Japan's impending surrender. This latter question was inseparably interwoven with the former. It is unrealistic to assume as Bernstein does, that one was more important than the other under the rapidly changing situations. It is more realistic to think that both intimidating the Soviet Union and bringing the war to a quick end without an invasion were equally important considerations within the top echelons of the Truman administration.

Given the fact that the A-bomb was considered to fulfil these two purposes simultaneously, it is difficult to prove one way or the other. We should note that the meaning attached to the A-bomb changed after the successful testing of the bomb at Alamogordo. After that, the Soviet Union's participation in the war was viewed as unnecessary. Truman and his top civilian and military advisors were clearly aware of it. Consequently, an exclusionary logic began to affect the decision-making process in an increasing degree. The bomb became a convenient and useful means to "kill two birds with one stone" : the immediate objective of ending the war as quickly as possible, at this point, would also realize the other complementary objective of excluding the Soviet Union from having a strong voice in the administration of occupied Japan as well as in the making of a new liberal international order. The bomb was expected to achieve these two objectives simultaneously.

Having said that, I would like to note the significant contribution that historians have made in broadening our understanding of the complicated issues of Truman's historic decision. In other words, the present state of the facts on this question seems to have produced a new level of scholarly consensus, that there existed two important motives behind Truman's decision to use the atomic bomb: early termination of the war without an invasion and intimidation of the Soviets to make them more manageable in worsening Soviet-American relations.

THE QUESTION OF ALTERNATIVES

The question of alternatives concerns : (1) a non-combat demonstration as a dramatic warning; (2) modification of the unconditional surrender demand and an explicit guarantee of the imperial system; (3) pursuit of Japan's peace initiatives; (4) awaiting the effect of the Soviet entry into the war; (5) reliance on heavy conventional bombing and a naval blockade.

Bernstein argues that American leaders before Hiroshima "easily rejected or never considered most of the so-called alternatives to the bomb."[5] Admitting that such might have been the case, we could nonetheless ask questions, for an analytical purpose, why they were not pursued instead of the bomb, and what might have happened if one or more had instead been pursued. By asking these questions we should be able to better understand, explain, and evaluate the use of the A-bomb in August, 1945.

In examining these alternatives we need to bear in mind the following three things. First, "revisionist historians" approached this question without explicitly considering the time element, the invasion plan of 1st November, 1945 thus adding confusion to the initial debate. The current issue here is whether Japan would have been brought to its knees before the invasion date. Truman wanted to avoid the planned invasion of 1st November, 1945. If the war had continued past the date, thousands of Americans would have died in the invasion. Truman did not want to face such a consequence for fear of domestic political backlash. Even worse for the Japanese, more bombs would have been dropped if Japan had continued its fighting past mid-August, 1945.

Second, the past arguments focused too much on the one condition of retaining the emperor system as a key to Japan's surrender before the scheduled Kyushu invasion. However, the Japanese surrender terms to be discussed included not just one but the other three (assumption by the imperial headquarters of responsibility for disarming and demobilizing the imperial forces, no occupation, and the delegation to the Japanese government of punishing war criminals). Inseparably related to this is an assessment of the impact of the two key elements (A-bomb or Soviet entry) upon the Japanese decision-making process that eventually led to the final acceptance of the Potsdam Declaration. Without this analysis any assessment of the A-bomb decision would be incomplete.

After examining these alternatives, Bernstein expresses "serious doubts that any single alternative would alone have produced surrender before the November invasion without the use of the A-bomb. Furthermore, in his estimate "a synergistic combination" of guaranteeing the emperor, awaiting Soviet entry, and continuing the heavy bombing of cities accompanied by the blockade would seem "very likely" to have ended the war in time to avoid the invasion. He also estimates that the impact of Soviet entry amid the blockade and the heavy aerial bombardments could "quite possibly" have accomplished that goal without dropping the atomic bomb.[6]

The problems with his reasoning is that he downplays the role of Soviet entry, so much so that he regards the continued heavy bombing of Japanese cities together with the naval blockade as having more impact on a surrender before 1st November than the Soviet entry. He tries to distinguish between "the fact" that American policy-makers did not believe the Soviet entry likely to be decisive and the post-Hiroshima analysis which suggests that Soviet entry might well have produced a surrender before the November invasion. Such a distinction is difficult to square with Truman's diary entry for 17th July, 1945 which reads "Finish Japs when that [Soviet entry] comes about." He also wrote in a letter to his wife on 18th July that he had "gotten what I came for—Stalin goes to war August 15 [and] we'll end the war a year sooner now, and think of kids who won't be killed."[7]

An examination of the Japanese decision-making process seems to confirm that the Soviet entry was as equally devastating to the Japanese ruling circles. The court group had a very strong sense of internal crisis: Lord Keeper of the Privy Seal Kido Koichi in the closing weeks of the war frequently met the chief of the Home Ministry's Police Bureau and the superintendent general of the Metropolitan Police while collecting the latest information about the deteriorating domestic situation from the commander of the Military Police. The Emperor Hirohito "agreed completely" with Prince Konoe Fumimaro's observation on 12th July, 1945 that "the situation today has reached the point where people hold a grudge against the imperial house." Navy Minister Yonal Mitsumasa said to his confidant Takagi Sokichi, on 12 August, that "the atomic bombs and the Soviet entry into the war are, in a sense, gifts from the gods. This way we don't have to say that we have quit the war because of domestic circumstances."[8] These leaders were increasingly worried about the revolutionary ferment that might endanger the imperial policy. The Soviet entry was a great shock because it seemed to them to make such an eventuality a realistic possibility. Moreover, to the proponents of peace such as Foreign Minister Togo Shigenori, it meant that their forlorn hope of Soviet good offices was completely gone. To the military diehards, it meant that their homeland battle strategy based on Moscow's neutrality sustained a severe blow, thus seriously undermining the theoretical and strategic basis for defending the military's position.[9]

The above examination of the Japanese decision-making process shows that both the A-bomb and the Soviet entry together produced Japan's surrender on 15th August, 1945. Therefore, I agree with Marquis Kido's statement that "if it had not been for the A-bomb and the Soviet entry into the war, it is doubtful whether the scheme to terminate the war would have been realized without much ado."

THE QUESTION OF JUSTIFICATION OR LEGITIMATIZATION

A Missed Opportunity

The "revisionist historians" raised the question of "a missed opportunity" by suggesting various alternatives to end the war without the A-bomb and without the November invasion. As was already discussed, Bernstein also has reached a conclusion that a synergistic combination of some of the alternatives would have ended the war in time to avoid the November invasion. The present state of the historiography cast a doubt on the contention that the bomb was necessary. From what now seems known, it is hard to be persuaded that the pre-Hiroshima processes of decision-making and analysis within the Truman administration were adequate in the light of the enormous costs exacted from the victims.

The Redefinition of Wartime Morality

Several studies noted the American air doctrine and how it transformed the wartime morality during the World War II. Ronald Schaffer pointed out that American airpower doctrine accepted the principle that in modern total war, civilians and armed forces were inseparably linked in national war machines and that "one way to break those machines was to smash civilian will."[10] The concept of strategic bombing marked the break with tradition in which war had been primarily against combatants, and the moral revulsion caused by indiscriminate killings of civilians in city bombings. American leaders—both political and military—were largely inured to the mass killing of civilians. Bernstein also notes that "that redefinition of morality" made Hiroshima and Nagasaki possible.[11] In other words, the dropping of the A-bomb was a culmination of the concept of strategic bombing and the resultant transformation of wartime morality. Thus the Target Committee, composed of Leslie Groves, army, air force men and scientists agreed to choose "large urban areas of not less than three miles in diameter existing in the larger populated area" as A-bomb targets. Of central importance for the group's consideration was to produce "the greatest psychological effect against Japan" and to make the world, and the Soviet Union in particular, aware that America possessed this new power.

These studies point up two things. First, it is important to note the fact that the transformation of the older morality-soldiers should seek to spare non-combatants—took place during the World War II. However, it does not mean that we should approve of it. Though we understand the historical context, we could and should question the moral foundation of this new concept of strategic bombing. John Rawls stresses that the "two nihilistic doctrines" must be repudiated. One of these is the kind of nihilism expressed by General William Sherman's remark, "War is hell," so any means can be justified to end the war as soon as possible. Rawls argues that "just and decent civilized societies depend absolutely on taking significant moral and political distinctions in all situations." "There is never a time," according to him, "when we are free from all moral and political principles and restraints."[12]

Second, the emergence of this new moral climate that justifies indiscriminate killings and the wide acceptance of it among American leaders clearly reveal that America was not morally unique but just technologically superior. When they had the bomb, they simply used it just like Japan and Germany would have used it. There were few moral restraints left among them. The US atrocities and war crimes in the Vietnam War as symbolically revealed in the My Lai massacre of 1968 only confirmed it. The massive killings of the enemy population both by dropping the A-bomb and through the massive aerial bombing during the Vietnam War have much in common with each other, revealing the savagery of modern war. These traumatic events together continue to have an enduring impact on American society and culture by throwing a doubt on the traditional American creed, the foundation of America's exceptionalism.

Having said that, there is no reason to believe, we should hasten to add, that the leaders or citizens of any of the major wartime countries including Japan and Germany would have sought to avoid dropping the bomb on the enemy and its non-combatants. In addition, the concept of area bombing as well as that of total war was shared by the other powers.

The Italians bombed Ethiopian villages, Germans obliterated part of Rotterdam, and V-2s were fired to kill anyone they landed on, the Japanese indiscriminately bombed Chinese cities. Not to mention of Germany's systematic murder of six million Jews and Japan's rape of Nanking.

The Strange Myth of 500,000 Casualties

Many Americans continue to believe even today that the use of the A-bomb was necessary, desirable and justifiable. The main reasons for such thinking are based, first, on their belief that the bomb brought the end of the war, and second, on their popular notion that 500,000 to 1 million American lives were saved by the termination of the war before the two scheduled invasions on 1st November, 1945 and in the spring of 1946. As for the first point, we already made it clear that the role of the bomb must be evaluated vis-à-vis the role the Soviet entry into the war played as well as by putting the A-bomb decision in a larger historical context including a careful and full examination of various other alternatives. As for the second point, the recent historiography abundantly made clear that the 500,000 American casualties figure estimated and propagated by Truman and others is a myth. The present consensus among historians about the estimated loss of American lives in the invasions is 40,000-45,000. James B. Conant, Harvard's president and a wartime atomic policy-maker, Karl T. Compton, MIT's president and wartime atomic energy advisor, Henry Stimson, Truman and others were fearful of doubts and criticism emerging in America about the A-bomb decisions and tried to shape popular understanding of the decision to their liking.[13] Their efforts to "create the right history" produced this myth of 500,000-1 million American casualties. The uncovering of this myth significantly undercuts the American top policy-makers' justifications and seriously challenges that part of the nation's collective memory that the bomb saved many American lives.

PERCEPTION GAPS AND COLLECTIVE MEMORY

The cancellation of the National Air and Space Museum's original Enola Gay exhibition in January 1995 and the controversy triggered by this plan are a clear testimony to the existence of wide gaps between Japanese and American perceptions of the A-bomb decision. The polls conducted in September 1995 by the NHK Hoso Bunka Kenkyusho confirm the gap. 57.8 per cent of the Japanese respondents thought that the use of the bomb was wrong. Those who thought its use was justified constituted only 8.2 per cent. On the other hand, 62.3 per cent of the Americans thought its use was right, and only 25.7 per cent thought its use was wrong.

By way of narrowing these perception gaps between Americans and Japanese, we need to deepen our mutual understanding of World War II, and the Asia-Pacific War in particular. Many Americans have an image of World War II as a "good war" or a "just war". According to the gallup polls of January 1991, 89 per cent of the Americans thought that World War II was a "just war" while only 25 per cent of them thought that the Vietnam War was a "just war". On the other hand, the revulsion against war in general among the Japanese is widespread. Their attitude is one of "No more war". Many Japanese think that the Asia-Pacific War was a war of aggression and that Japan should apologize for it and pay compensation for the wartime victims. Recently, however, we can also observe the rise of nationalism in general and, kenbei in particular, among Japanese. In this new nationalistic trend, conservative politicians differentiate between their attitude towards the Japanese-American war and that towards the war in Asia. They think Japan need not apologize for the war against the United States because it was a war among the imperialist powers. On the other hand, they think Japan should apologize for the Asians against whom a war of aggression was waged.[14]

These perception gaps have so far trapped the peoples of the two countries in the "victim-victimizer syndrome" and the habit of mutual recrimination. Many Japanese feel that the US government should apologize for the dropping of the A-bomb. To this many Americans react negatively, saying that Japan should apologize for the attack on Pearl Harbour as well as its wartime atrocities. To break out of this impasse, the Japanese should make more efforts to convey a clear message to the Americans that Japan was responsible for initiating the attacks against the US and express a sincere apology for the wartime atrocities. On the other hand, Americans need to be more free from their ethnocentric 'view of the war or the just war' tradition.

The foregoing review of the recent historiography on the decision to use the A-bomb delineates an area of the scholarly consensus on the issues involved, suggesting a possibility of promoting mutual understanding between the two nations. First, the scholarly consensus maintains that included in Truman's motives for the A-bomb decision are not only the early termination of the war and saving of many American lives but also intimidation of the Soviets to make them more manageable in the US struggle to make a postwar international order in their own image. Second, the Truman orthodoxy's claim that 500,000-1 million American lives would have been saved by dropping the bomb is now repudiated. Third, the scholarly consensus further holds that the A-bomb was not the only means of ending the war by the November invasion but there were other alternatives available at that time. Fourth, in light of the emerging scholarly consensus, such a simplistic popular notion that the use of the A-bomb was "necessary, desirable, and easily justifiable" need to be revised. Historians can play a role in this direction and make a contribution to a better understanding of the controversial issues involved in Truman's decisions. To that end, I would like to suggest one thing.

One of the principal means of informing collective memory is history textbooks. Samuel Walker, a historian at the US Nuclear Regulatory Commission concludes, after examining American school textbooks, that many American history textbooks "sustain myths about and questionable explanations for the use of the bomb." The treatment of the A-bomb decision by many textbooks are "regrettably flawed." He claims that it "reflects the historiography of the mid-1970s and fails to consider or include new findings."[15] Following Walker's example, a comparative look at some of the recently published works in Japan shows that we can reach a similar conclusion.

A 1995 publication by one of the leading Japanese historians on the A-bomb decision writes as follows: "In the 1970s .....it looks the revisionist thesis has been established. Today, insofar as the academic community is concerned, the thesis of early-termination-of-the-war/saving-many-American-lives is almost discredited." Compare this description with that of Walker's. Walker summarizes the existing state of the American historiography as follows: "The consensus of the mid-1970s, which held that the bomb was used primarily for military reasons and secondarily for diplomatic ones, continues to prevail. It has been challenged and reassessed in some of its specific points. But the central theme in the consensus that has existed for the past dozen years—that US officials always assumed that the bomb would be used and saw no reason not to use it once it became available—remains intact."[16] It seems to me that Japanese textbooks or scholarly works should be rewritten to reflect Walker's summary except for one thing. Though Walker's summarization is generally accurate, his secondary/primary distinction on Truman's motives need be more fully documented. My present position is that both factors weighed almost equally in Truman's decision to use the A-bomb. Bernstein's "bonus" thesis is hard to accept. The successful testing of the atomic bomb not only deprived American policy-makers of their incentive to pressure the Soviets to enter the war but they increasingly wished the Soviets would not come in. From that point on, intimidation of the Soviets was increasingly incorporated as an integral, essential part of the reason for using the bomb.

Another example can be drawn from Yui's book, an incisive collection of essays pondering on postwar US-Japan relations. He comments as follows: "We can now say that even no conservative historian will gulp down Truman's own explanation that the bomb was dropped to bring the war to an early end and to lessen the casualties of American soldiers that would have been expected by the landing operations against the Japanese homeland."[17] This description is flawed because it is misleading: Yui's explanation cannot convey to the reader that saving American soldiers' lives was a highly important consideration in the minds of Truman and his top policy makers. Neither will the reader be able to learn from this statement that early termination of the war without an invasion, for that matter, was a top priority for them.

A third example is an explanation given by Walker that reads as follows: "The consensus among scholars is that the bomb was not needed to avoid an invasion of Japan and to end the war within a relatively short time. It is clear that alternatives to the bomb existed and that Truman and his advisors knew it... it bears repeating that an invasion was a remote possibility."[18] Exposing and recognizing alternatives to the bomb is very important in unsettling popular misconceptions but Walker's explanation is insufficient in two respects. His emphasis that "an invasion was a remote possibility" cannot be substantiated if one looks into the Japanese decision-making process. He fails to consider the fierce struggle between the military die-hards and the peace-advocates over surrender terms. Also, we need to distinguish between what now seems known and what was believed before Hiroshima. From our present day perspective, we can question the adequacy of the pre-Hiroshima processes of decision-making and analysis in Washington. In light of the existing state of historiographical research, however, we also should convey to the reader that Truman did not carefully considered other alternatives. He and his advisors seem to have assumed that the bomb would be used once it became available.

Differences in explanations and interpretations remain among scholars. However, the chasm between scholarly views and collective memory seems much greater and more serious. This gap could be narrowed if scholars and popular historians would incorporate new findings and their implications into their writings about the use of the bomb. An obstacle to such efforts is greater in Japan at the secondary school level because school textbooks must be authorized by the Ministry of Education, one of the powerful sources of "history with a purpose." The Ministry's attempt to rewrite history bears symbolic testimony that collective memory will remain poorly informed with the distorted justifications and popular misconceptions being largely intact, unless historians make strenuous efforts to inform the public of what really happened concerning the use of the bomb.

REFERENCES

1. Herbert Feis, *Japan Subdued: The Atomic Bomb and the End of the War in the Pacific*, Princeton UP, 1961. The revised edition, *The Atomic Bomb and the End of World War II*, Princeton UP, 1966, Geofrey Warner, "To End a War: The Decision to Drop the Bomb", in David Carlton and Herbert M. Levine eds., *The Cold War Debate*, McGraw-Hill Co., 1988, 34-39.
2. Gar Alperovitz, *Atomic Diplomacy*, Vintage Books, 1965. An expanded edition, Penguin Books, 1985. A revised edition, Pluto Press, 1994. See also the following works by the same author: *The Decision to Use the Atomic Bomb*, The Exploratory Project for Economic Alternatives, 1994; "Hiroshima: Historians Reasess," *Foreign Policy* (Summer 1995). Gar Alperovitz and Robert Messer, "Marshall, Truman, and the Decision to Drop the Bomb", *International Security* 16 (Winter 1991/92). Gar Alperovitz and Kai Bird, "The Centrality of the Bomb." *Foreign Policy* (Spring 1994). Robert L. Messer, "New Evidence on Truman's Decision." *Bulletin of the Atomic Scientists* 41 (August 1985).
3. Barton J. Bernstein, "Roosevelt, Truman and the Atomic Bomb, 1941-1945: A Reinterpretation," *Political Science Quarterly* 90 (Spring 1975); "The Perils and Politics of Surrender: Ending the War with Japan and Avoiding the Third Atomic Bomb," *Pacific Historical Review* p. 56 (February 1977); "The Atomic Bombings Reconsidered," *Foreign Affairs* (January/February 1995); "Understanding the Atomic Bomb and the Japanese Surrender," *Diplomatic History* (Spring 1995).
4. Feis, 1996 *op. cit.*, pp. 194-95. Martin J. Sherwin, *A World Destroyed*, Knopf, 1975. c. 1973; "The Atomic Bomb and the Origins of the Cold War," *The American Historical Review* (October 1993), 945-68; "Old Issues in New

Editions," *Bulletin of the Atomic Scientists* 41 (December 1985). Bernstein, "Eclipsed by Hiroshima and Nagasaki," *International Security* 15 (Spring 1991), 169-70.

5. Bernstein, "Understanding the Atomic Bomb and the Japanese Surrender," *op. cit*, 235.
6. *Ibid.*, 254.
7. Truman, "Potsdam Diary," 18 July 1945. Truman to Bess, 18 July 1945, Truman Papers.
8. Gaimusho ed., *Shusenshiroku*, Shinbun Gekkansha, 1952, pp. 195-98. Kurihara Ken and Hatano Sumio eds., *Shusen Kosaku no Kiroku*, Vol. 1, Kodansha, 1986, pp. 482-85. Takagi Sokichi, *Takagi Kaigun Shosho Oboegaki*, Mainichi Shimbunsha, 1979, p. 351.
9. Yoshida Yutaka, *Shova Tenno no Shusenshi*, Iwanami Shoten, pp. 28-30. Tanaka Nobumasa, *Dokyumento Showa Tenno*, vol. 5, Ryokufu Shuppan, 1988, pp. 460-61, 475-76. Hideki Kan, The A-Bomb, Soviet Entry, and Japan's Surrender," *Kitakyushu Daigaku Kaigaku 25-Shunen Ronbunshu* (December 1972), 369-79. Herber Bix, "Japan's Delayed Surrender: A Reinterpretation," *Diplomatic History* (Spring 1995), pp. 218-19. Bix estimates that "massive conventional bombing alone, or in combination with a Soviet declaration of war," would have forced Japan's surrender before the invasion *(Ibid.*, p. 218, note 63).
10. Ronald Schaffer, *Wings of Judgment*, Oxford UP, 1985, p. 33. See also, Michael S. Sherry, *The Rise of American Air Power*, Yale UP, 1987, pp. 152-54, 260-61.
11. Bernstein, "The Atomic Bombing Reconsidered," *op. cit.*, 151-52.
12. John Rawls's article in "Fifty Years after Hiroshima: Symposium," *Dissent* (Summer 1995), p. 327.
13. Rufus E. Miles, "Hiroshima: The Strange Myth of Half a Million American Lives Saved," *International Security* 10 (Fall 1985). Barton J. Bernstein, "A Postwar Myth: 500,000 U.S. Lives Saved," *Bulletin of the Atomic Scientists* (June/July 1986). Bernstein, "Writing, Righting, or Wrong doing the Historical Record," *Diplomatic History* 16 (Winter 1992). Bernstein, "Seizing the Contested Terrain of Early Nuclear History," *Diplomatic History* 17 (Winter 1993). James G. Hershberg, *James B. Conant: Harvard to Hiroshima and the Making of the Nuclear Age*, Knopf, 1993. Paul Boyer, *By the Bomb's Early Light,* The University of North Carolina Press, 1994, pp. 196-203.
14. Studs Turkel, *The Good War: An Oral History of World War II*, Ballantine Books, 1984. Ian Buruma, *Wages of Guilt: Memories of War in Germany and Japan*, Farrar, Straus and Glroux, 1994. Yui Daizaburo, *Nichibel Sensokan no Sokoku*, Iwanami Shoten, 1995, pp. 35-48. Asada Sadao, "The Mushroom Cloud and National Psyches: Japanese and American Perceptions of the A-bomb Decision, 1945-1995," *Journal of American-East Asian Relations* (Summer 1995).
15. J. Samuel Walker, "History, Collective Memory, and the Decision to Use the Bomb," *Diplomatic History* 19 (Spring 1995), 326.

16. Arai Shinichi, *Sensou Sekinin*, Iwanami Shoten, 1995, p. 215. See also the same author's book *Genbaku Toka e no Michi*, Tokyo Daigaku Shuppankai, 1985. J. Samuel Walker, "The Decision to Use the Bomb: A Historiographical Update," *Diplomatic History* 16 (Winter 1990), 111.
17. Yui, *op. cit.*, p. 13.
18. Walker, "The Decision to Use the Bomb," *op. cit.*, 110.
19. This paper was presented at the Hiroshima Symposium: entitled Fifty years of Nuclear Weapons Revisited at Hiroshima Prefectural Cultural Center on September 17-18, 1996.

3

Nuclear Weapons and end of the Cold War

Hiroharu Seki*

The author in this article has emphasized the importance of the "new mode of thinking" among decision-makers not only of the US and USSR (now Russia) but also of other powers as well as small countries to create a nuclear weapon-free world. He is fundamentally critical of such theory that the change of the mode of thinking will progress automatically. New ideas have to be evolved for an alternative road to nuclear disarmament which is totally different from nuclear deterrence. Moreover, "deconstruction of traditional knowledge structure is not enough to create non-nuclear world", he has argued.

Nevertheless, it is very difficult in the traditional network of power politics to evolve new ideas.

Nuclear weapons have been one of the biggest global issues for the past 50 years. The issues were sometimes manifest depending on the political situations of related powers and regions, but most of times the issues were latent and hidden. The latter cases were often the outcome of the information controls manipulated by some hidden media organized by the military-industrial-academic complex of the related powers.[1] Most of those cases have tended to produce complicated political processes. One of the illustrative such cases were the political complexity of the return of Okinawa to Japan in 1972 after 27 years of American occupation of the islands. Detailed process of that complexity was partly but well

* The author is Director of Institute of International Relations and Area studies, Ritsumeikan University, Japan.

explained by the late Wakaizumi's book, published one year before his death by cancer, entitled *Tasaku Nakarishi wo Shinzento Hossu* (Wanting to Believe in No Alternative Policy).

A complex process like the return of Okinawa to Japan, which I have mentioned above, could not be created by the static structure of the global system itself. As a whole, it has been created as a salient aspect of complexity to be explored only by their fundamental characteristics which include subjective-objective nexus between decision-makers and other broadly related agents. The process itself is not a linear extension of the original point. If we follow the general terminology of the principle of complexity, it should be emphasized that very frequently non-linear extension might take us to the chaos type of destination even in the mathematical formulation[2]. It means that thc destination is not predictable in the deterministic paradigm. This is the fundamental difference between Cartesian Newtonian formulation and the formulation by the Santa Fe type of complexity paradigm.

We have another approach to the complexity of the global system itself. The reality that each simple systems such as Westphalian system, borderless capitalist type of interdependence system and subjectivity oriented dominance-dependence type of vertical system, which are only three salient examples of the global complexity, produces one complex system of our world, would surely show us that those simple systems should have linkages among them even if those linkage structures could not be well identified[3].

Our approach to the global system to explore the end of the cold war in the dynamic paradigm is epistemologically too difficult to be empirically studied. However, once we look at the process ontologically and subjectively, it is often not so difficult. The reason is that once we want to analyse it pragmatically, the difficulty could be solved by the supremacy of the higher level of political leadership to which any individual could show his or her identity. Structure of knowledge, in spite of its complexity, would be easily deconstructed in the preference of politics to the structure of knowledge.

Our approach to the exploration of how nuclear weapons were related to the end of the cold war should include our political will of moral leadership as one of the most significant variables. It means that without the preference of ontology to epistemology or without the preference of subjectivity to objectivity in the ontological-epistemological linkage structures, we cannot initiate the road towards solving any kind of the global problematic. Why it is so transferred from the study of global gaming type exercise different from all computer simulation like GLOBUS.[4]

Another type of solution is the Ju Che type of philosophy created by the late Kim Il Sung of the Democratic Peoples Republic of Korea (DPRK) in which the will of the leadership created the collectivity-oriented human centered philosophy.[5] If we could characterize American pragmatism as the individualism-oriented human-centered philosophy, ironical homomorphism between American pragmatism and Korean Ju Che could be explored even in the end of the cold war in Asia. Recent negotiation between the US and the DPRK around the nuclear issues, which successfully created the Korean Energy Development Organization (KEDO), is a good subject of case study for both philosophies.

NUCLEAR STRATEGY AS AN INTELLECTUAL GENE

In my previous article, "Pearl Harbour, Hiroshima and World Order"[6], I tried to explicate the concept of intellectual development gene which has been extracted from Pearl Harbour-Hiroshima linkage in the military strategic paradigm. Whether it would be an evil gene or normal gene should be rather explored in the context of global history as a super-complexity level of political, economic and cultural process of interaction and interpenetration from the cold war to the post-cold war periods.

It is quite natural that hermeneutics of such global history tends to raise serious disputes among historians specialized in the beginning of the cold war as well as the end of the cold war. The most salient example is John Lewis Gaddis's chapter in one of PRIO's publications "Nuclear Rivalry and International Order" edited by Jorn Gjelstad and Olav Njolstad. In Chapter 4[7] of that book, Gaddis rather admires nuclear deterrence policy as quite successful specially in the crisis situation in the sense that nuclear weapons are so different from previous weapons that future national interests of any country including the superior supernuclear powers such as the US or previous USSR could not be assured in the decision-maker's perspective.

Gaddis's evaluation is based on the so-called long peace after the World War II as compared with the war-ridden previous periods. But, the factors contributed to long peace would be more complex than the simple explanation by the logic of Westphalian network. Gaddis's explanation is more close to the equilibrium theory of Neo-Classical Economics[8] without mentioning much about the system of complexity developed by Santa Fe Research Institute. And in the cold war periods, there were Korean War, Vietnam War, Middle Eastern Wars and other several wars which killed astonishingly high numbers of non-combatants although the World War III was narrowly escaped in the marginal edge. Gaddis's optimistic evaluation of the nuclear deterrence policy would be a superpower-based ontological thinking characterized as the following axiom. "Fools are wise after the events".

Gaddis's type of thinking tells us a similar type of reasoning that Japan's Pacific war was a just war for emancipation because Japanese military occupation emancipated the Western colony from Western Imperialism and most of the present Asian countries have become independent thanks to Japan's War against Western powers in which the US took a leading role. Of course, Gaddis emphasizes that the invention of nuclear weapons did fundamentally change our mode of thinking contrary to the remarks of Albert Einstein and John Mueller.

I don't want to explain what is the main cause of the schism and difference between Gaddis and Einstein or between Gaddis and Mueller here. The simple answer might be the difference of the ontological position and of the quasi-independent epistemological structure, among three, which integratedly produce different moral standards in the global theory and history.

Going back to the concept of intellectual gene created by the strategic aspects of Pearl Harbour-Hiroshima linkage, originally I characterized Japan's attack on Pearl Harbour as Japan's necessity of conducting war against the US at least gainfully for a while based on the pure framework of military strategic logic. This logic is totally transferred to the so-called US Nuclear Utilization Strategy (NUTS) policy after the World War II. But, in this case of the US military strategic logic, it was more oriented towards the hypothetical reality, that is, "virtual reality" frequently used by the contemporary multimedia computer terminology. It should be especially pointed out here that NUTS was always hidden to the public even if it was integrated with so-called Mutual Assured Destruction (MAD) strategy which was popularly accepted even in the public relations in Hiroshima where the core part of the Peace Constitution of Japan was deeply rooted.

It could not be denied that the US decision-maker's objective experience of observing the horrible destruction and evaporation of Hiroshima by the nuclear explosion on the pity non-combatant children and women who lived there has become the basis of the concept of MAD strategy. It means that the MAD strategy was transferred to the cold war periods from Hiroshima. It would be well compared with the NUTS strategy transferred from Pearl Harbour more subjectively rather than objectively. So MAD-NUTS linkage always seems to have worked harmoniously in spite of the significant difference between the perspective of nuclear strategists inside as well as outside of Pentagon.

However, by the end of 1970s both types of nuclear strategies produced unstable and insoluble schism between them because of the rapid technological breakthrough leading to the development of missiles such as MaRV (Manoeuvreable Re-entry Vehicle). It was a new reality in the sense that a new nuclear arms race started in the end of 1970's. Thus, the Reagan era was vividly characterized as the highest point of nuclear arms race between the US and the former USSR. MAD-NUTS controversy had created the virtual reality of nuclear crisis in the circle of decision-makers of the US. On the other hand, subjective response around the issues of morality and the resultant peace movement, which began in Europe, was strongly ignited. Such response was not the virtual reality rather it was the true reality accelerated by the NUTS strategy around the issues of deployment of Medium Range Ballistic Missile (MRBM) in Europe.

Interpenetration of schism and dilemma among nuclear strategists with issues of morality by humanity-oriented scholars and with massive peace movement which was originally ignited at Hiroshima created new terminologies such as Euroshima and Ameroshima. The centre of the peace movement suddenly moved to the place where was unquestionably the native place of the MAD-NUTS controversy from Hiroshima. It must be again specially noted here that the new reality was rather ignited by the speech of the Roman Catholic Pope who visited the United Nations University (UNU) in Tokyo and the City of Nagasaki. Pope's visit to Japan and the continuous invitation to the Palme Commission to visit the UNU and the city of Hiroshima through the cooperative efforts by the UNU, Hiroshima University[9] and the city of Hiroshima realized in 1981 on the eve of the reopening of the cold war.[10] It was an igniting start to reactivate the new type of thinking remarked by Einstein in May 1946, the period before the cold war. The reactivated new type of thinking surely pointed at the responsibilities of scientists and engineers. The idea continuous to this thinking supported the new way of action to publish "Common Security" as well as the Pastoral letter from Chicago Catholic Church respectively in 1982 and 1983 during which peace movements in Europe and in America continuously reached the highest stage which had never been experienced in human history.

Reagan's policy was forced to adapt to this situation as the top leader of the US Chameleon like. The result was Reagan's declaration to devise and develop new weapons such as Strategic Defence Initiative (STD). President Reagan was forced to change his previous view. That he himself declared in Japanese Diet that the war to permit the use of nuclear weapons would be the evil was as same as the declaration by the Pastoral Letter. Of course, there was a continuation of his tough policy against the USSR based on the SDI. And it also inspired counter argument against the SDI as reasoning it a fantasy. Ironically, those critical strategists against Reagan were mobilized by Harvard University. It published the critical book against the Pastoral Letter to emphasize the nuclear deterrence as a necessity. *Living with Nuclear Weapons* edited by Bog, Harvard President, was such a book to which Joseph Nye also contributed. On the other hand, Gorbachev quickly responded to the *Common Security* edited by Olaf Palme who visited Hiroshima. It was the Perestroika which began in 1985 immediately after he assumed power in the USSR. How the intellectual gene of MAD-NUTS linkage type of strings changed in this development of creative adaptation by the both political leaders to the new way of thinking? This is the analytical story more oriented towards the principle of complexity.

Gaddis's type of reasoning for long peace in the cold war periods is simple system oriented. It is based on the equilibrium type of theory in Westphalian network without subjective will of the people all over the world to end the cold war irrespective of the fundamental characteristics of the Westphalian system. The process of the cold war as long peace is very questionable in the sense of complexity theory. I must here point to the US-Japan relations after the World War II as the torsional history in the sense that in spite of the de-Westphalianized character of Japanese Peace Constitution, the US decision-makers always criticized Japanese intellectuals of being too naive for watching the wolf-ridden international politics. Of course, the late Masao Maruyama resisted this argument by emphasizing the end of the cold war as necessary if we want to forecast the long term strategic interests of the both camps. Such explanation was totally the same as Einstein's thinking. And it was written by Maruyama in June 1950 *(Mitabi Heiwa ni Tsuite,* Third Joint Statement on Problems of Peace, in Monthly Magazine *Sekai).* I already explained the details of his argument in my book entitled *Asia Pacific in the Global Transformation* published in 1987 when the neorealist type of gloomy objectivism still prevailed in Japan. [11]

RETHINKING THE POST-COLD WAR

The post-cold war period was interpreted as the 'End of History' by Francis Fukuyama. It was totally oriented to the victory of liberal ideology based on the market economy without thinking about nuclear crisis in the 1980's. MAD-NUTS controversy from the end of 1970's was not mentioned in his argument. It could not be denied that market economy was successful in the Western World particularly in thc Asia Pacific and the Soviet type of planned economy failed to compete with the market economy particularly in the spheres of mass consumption and mass production for consumers. In this sense, Gorbachev's idea of Perestroika was only successful towards the end of the cold war but in the revised form of transference of market economy based on the continuation of planned economy, Gorbachev totally failed to reconstruct and reform the Soviet economic system.

Apparent superiority of the market economy in the Western Europe over the planned economy of the Eastern Europe controlled by the USSR has not only obscured the fundamental meaning of socialism which originated in the West in the 19th century but also dissipated the issues around the nuclear strategy deeply rooted in the historical Westphalian system. The meaning of such a situation in the post-cold war period is that the military security-oriented Westphalian characteristics remained even after the cold war ended in spi te of the radical political and economic change of the global system, particularly in the previous Soviet bloc. Thus, the nuclear deterrence policy of the five nuclear powers has also continued till today when issues around the negotiation over CTBT are in a deadlock. In spite of our clear understanding that the threats from nuclear proliferation are acknowledged by all concerned decision-makers, the Indian policy was adamant to reject CTBT by her conditional demand to ask the five nuclear powers to set the deadline for the abolition of nuclear weapons. To tell its implication, here is deeply hidden the controversy around the issues of continuation of nuclear deterrence policy by the super-nuclear powers like the US even after the cold war ended[12].

In the post-cold war period, most of the specialists in peace studies as well as those in international relations expected to see a better world than in the period of the cold war. However, ethnic conflicts and the conflicts arising from competition among different nationalims were intensified not only in the third world but also in the Western developed world. Even in the United States, there is a definite and strong tendency to the rising ethnic conflicts among groups of different origin. The situation promoted the revival of the traditional type of security thinking by big powers irrespective of the once agreed concept of common security in the last stage of the second cold war period. Even in Japan, Peace Constitution is more and more neglected when faced with the new political situations in the Asia Pacific region. Among the security specialists of the US and Japan, several issues around the military security of regions such as Taiwan strait and Korean peninsula are being raised around the future role of China as the big power as well as around the continuous severe conflicts between North Korea and South Korea as divided nations by superpowers.

Here again, the revival of the traditional military strategic thinking, based on the combination of security-oriented military action and the geopolitical way of thinking, tends to prevail in the revised new definition of the US-Japan security pact, as compared with the rising tendency of alternative ideas such as geoeconomic thinking which could rather promote the new regional cooperation among previously antagonistic areas and nations. The latter tendency, if it prevails, would be expected to overcome the military strategic aspects of traditional deterrence policy and to strengthen the common security idea by accelerating the creative diplomatic actions as illustrated by Jimmy Carter's visit to the DPRK in 1994.

The question of how nuclear weapons were related to the end of the cold war is again picked up to analyze this complicated process in the Asia Pacific region particularly in the North-East Asia within the new paradigm of the creative action to the deepening and expanding Asia Pacific era. Of course, in Europe, the Finland model was salient to bringing an end to the cold war. This is well illustrated by the formation of CSCE process in whole Europe. Why the same kind of CSCA process as the CSCE process in Europe could not be created in the Asia Pacific region in spite of the end of the cold war in the global scale?[13] This is the significant question to be answered. A simple answer rather tends to explain the strength of nationalism in the Asia Pacific region particularly in this global political periphery which had been the victim of the extension of the Westphalian system by the skillful learning of power politics by Japan and the US for the past hundred years. The process of such learning is well illustrated in Japan's entry into the Western world and the US learning from Pearl Harbour and Hiroshima—both of which are mutual learning processes for the military strategic doctrine in the form of intermingled interpenetration. I already explained such phenomena of the mutual learning process in my historical study of transfer of military strategic idea as the new intellectual gene. But, it is a very complicated process to rethink over such concepts as applicable to the Asia Pacific region.

Here, we must rethink over the Finland model on the higher dimension of complexity theory. It must be pointed out that we are not criticizing the Finland model as Finlandization which of course is a bad terminology enough to induce rejection of the transfer of Finland policy into security groups like NATO or the US-Japan security pact in the cold war period. But, we are rather wanting to describe Finland model in its clear limitation necessary to be reconsidered. The limitation of that model is being well recognized in the new violent conflicts illustrated in Bosnia and Serbia which should have been solved in the broader perspective of the extension of the CSCE process expected to be developed as a natural extension of the Finland model. Surely this process could not be realized. I recognized it clearly on the occasion of Ritsumeikan-American Joint Symposium held in Vienna in 1992 before the military conflicts in the region actually happened. In this case, the computer simulation which, Dr. Frances Mautner-Markhov, the principal organizer of the Vienna Symposium, developed in the applied form of conflict resolution towards the Korean case, could not applicable even to her native region in Europe.

We must add one significant episode to this symposium. Two of DPRK scholars came to the symposium for my invitation to the conference. But their participation in the conference was readily unaccepted for some unknown reasons. It was the process of complexity which Dr. Frances Markhov herself could not forecast beforehand. She was the scholar who has been attached to the IAEA and participated in the Korean Unification Conference held in Osaka. There she met both Korean high ranking scholars and politicians. The conference was held in 1990. Her simulation paper concentrated on the solution of Korean conflict which was also printed in a book published in Japan in 1991. It is very interesting to be analysed comparing with later period when Jimmy Carter started to make his effort to meet Kim Il Sung, DPRK's top leader. To the Osaka Conference Jimmy Carter sent a significant telegram to celebrate this occasion to be successful.

We must also recognize the new beginning of nuclear crisis between the US and DPRK in 1992. During the period between 1992 and 1994, the most complicated political process around the issue of nuclear energy development of DPRK was progressed. The proccss was extremely significant in the sense that the serious security problems for the North-East Asia was highly provocated particularly in Japan. Then the Jimmy Carter shock came to Japan because he was successful to talk to the great leader Kim Il Sung to solve the nuclear negotiation crisis two months before Kim Il Sung's death. Nuclear disarmament issues should also be analysed in this framework of negotiation between the US and DPRK.

Here our analysis must focus on the idea of Ju Che philosophy devised by late Kim II Sung. This looks like something totally different from the relationship between nuclear weapons and the end of the cold war. But it might be the most interesting and salient as well as complicated aspect to be explored in the study of the relationship between the end of the cold war in the Sea of Japan Rim[14] and the issues around the development of nuclear weapons by the previously non-nuclear country. Ju Che ideology strongly emphasizes that the global process is going to the direction in which human being could take the role of masters step by step. This is the process of evoking man's subjective consciousness to the creative self-consciousness, creativeness and self-independence.

The meaning is that the human being would become the masters of the globe in the collective learning network from which they could be born and be learnt as well as be grown. The collective process is not only physically identified but also emotionally and spiritually identified. It is surely the deconstructed form of Marxist philosophy. In this sense. American philosophy of pragmatism is very much similar to Ju Che philosophy except for the difference that the former is totally the son of Western individualism and the latter is also the daughter of the Marxist type of collectivism. Both were deconstructed from the original reasoning of the Western logic of epistemology because of the political emphasis towards pragmatic action-oriented solution of the insoluble dilemma in the world of knowledge.

How such comparison is useful would probably be well examined in the nuclear negotiation process between the US and DPRK to have reached the agreement for the new establishment of KEDO between the two countries, one as the super nuclear power and other as the previous small victim of the Westphalian logic badly learnt by the historical big powers including Japan as the aspirant to become the military leader in the Asia Pacific in the pre-World War II period. Thus the comparison between the Finland model and the DPRK model represented by Ju Che idea could be also salient towards the rethinking for the alternative creation of the future world order through which abolition of the nuclear weapons would be successfully achieved. Japan's Peace Constitution based on the ontological deep experience should be introduced in this type of world order formation. The intermediate order, which might be characterized as CSCA type of world order finally to transform the present order to the future non-nuclear world order, would be surely different from the CSCE type of world order. At present, the post-cold war period is not successful in creating the road to total nuclear disarmament, that is, abolition of the nuclear weapons.

Conclusion

The conclusion of my paper is mostly oriented to my criticism of Gaddis's way of reasoning for "the protracted long peace" under the nuclear deterrence theory of cold war period. This criticism is mainly based on the combination of alternative ontological and hermeneutic interpretation in history and the theoretical revolution from the simplicity type of reasoning based on the equilibrium theory to the complexity type of reasoning which should include the internal subjective will in the complexity network as a necessary evolutional condition. The origin of such reasoning was the Ilya Prigogine's alternative entropy theory as well as the Albert Einstein's new mode of thinking just opposite to Gaddis's reasoning and his conclusion.

At first, Gaddis's long peace is not the protracted long peace during which stability was set without unstable nuclear crisis. It was rather the period during which the total human life on our planet and the human civilization on our globe might be eradicated. In our symbolic expression, everything was closed in "the so-called Doomsday Machine" by the logical conclusion of the US-USSR nuclear rivalry. Why it could be defined as stable peace without strong possibility of the final breakdown of the states of equilibrium which was supposed to be the same type of logical outcome as explained in neoclassical economics? If it would be the stable peace, we must ask why the end of the cold war was necessary. There was no reason to end the cold war period.

Secondly, Gaddis emphasized the importance of the new mode of thinking among decision-makers not only in the US and USSR but also of other powers as well as small countries. However, even if the mode of thinking of salient decision-makers changed when faced with nuclear crisis, we are fundamentally critical of such theory that the change of the mode of thinking progressed automatically without thinking about internal struggle for creating new idea to open alternative road to the nuclear disarmament which is totally different from the nuclear deterrence. The new principles were ideas such as the common security and the responsibilities of scientists and engineers. Gaddis's explanation has not even a weak validity. This is also the outcome of our different hermeneutics to interpret history from the cold war to the post-cold war period.

Thirdly, this paper is also very critical of Gaddis's explanation of automatic change of decision-maker's mode of thinking when faced with nuclear crisis including the US or USSR as well as decision-makers of the other nuclear states and non-nuclear states in addition to the leaders of peace movement and intellectual critics. Peace research leaders' ideological and theoretical conflicts with power elites were the very significant sources of change based on the salient individuals' efforts to create alternative intellectual networks in which universities, think tanks, religious organizations in addition to the minority global critical intellectuals would take a transformational leadership for the innovation of knowledge structure and alternative political decision for traditional nuclear policy based on the Westphalian characteristics. In this situation, Hiroshima and Peace Constitution of Japan would become an ontological basis for the new mode of thinking not only based on the direct feeling of the atomic bomb victims but also based on the alternative theory creation.

Weakness of the Japanese spiritual mode is characterized by totally separate two styles, that is, belief in direct feeling or belief in dead theory. These characteristics were clearly illustrated and then criticised by the most creative late Japanese political scientist, Masao Maruyama who was also an atomic bomb survivor in Hiroshima in August 6, 1945. He visited Hiroshima in 1977 for the first time after he was forced to experience the horrible atomic bomb blast as a soldier in Hiroshima. It was two years after the establishment of the Institute of Peace Science attached to the Hiroshima University as the first Peace Research Institute in Japan. Even his creative thinking could not integrate his idea around the issues of Hiroshima with his theoretical thinking although he wrote the most challenging article "Mitabi Heiwani Tsuite". That might be the main reason why he accepted my invitation to visit the Institute for Peace Science for his lecture on historical perspective. Following his splendid lecture at the Institute of Peace Science in 1977, I want to make a new proposal for the alternative research such as to set up in this symposium following Imre Lakotos' familiar terminology explained in his edited book entitled *Criticism and Growth of Knowledge*[15].

Moreover, I am thinking that deconstruction of traditional knowledge structure is not enough to create a non-nuclear world. Significant alternative political decision is also necessary. But it is very difficult in the traditional network of power politics. We must create an alternative network different from Westphalian type of power network. In various types of such creative network formation some of such networks could surely contribute to alternative political decision. Alternative political decision would be formed by the complexity principle which could clearly describe the delicate type of "entropy" decreasing process, even in the Westphalian network. In the total network, the innovative transformational activities by creative intellectual by these alternative networks would be, step by step, realized. This is not the direct products of knowledge structure, but the products of the political will and political action through deep learning of the alternative knowledge structure. The most illustrative case even in the post-cold war period in Europe was the ex-US President, Jimmy Carter's visit to Pyongyang in the crisis situation of the US-DPRK negotiation for solving nuclear issues between the two countries.

How to relate this individual creativity by Jimmy Carter to the nuclear issues in the post-cold war era, should be also picked up for exploring the NPT regime and newly developing issues around the CTBT. Has nuclear deterrence policy still any validity? Or, should it be discarded quickly? When Pastoral Letter was published in 1983 in the midst of the intensified crisis of US-USSR nuclear confrontation, the same kind of question was raised by the dispute between Pastoral Letter and "The Living with Nuclear Weapons" published by the Harvard University. What about this dispute in the reformed level of the post- cold war period? Why the traditional type of concept of common nation states and the concept of old-fashioned national security is still workable in this revolutionary period of technological innovation? It is the most important question to be answered for the total abolition of nuclear weapons. An automatic process to new mode of thinking could not be realized without the deep struggle for rethinking. Otherwise, the road to a new mode of thinking as mentioned by Albert Einstein might become a daytime dream. Gaddis's assertion that the new mode of thinking was automatically formed is questionable and groundless.

REFERENCES

1. Eric Mlyn, the State, Society, and Limited Nuclear War, State University of New York Press, 1995; Mlyn explains such hidden aspects of the nuclear policy of the US by highlighting the role of domestic politics and the relationship among three levels of policy, that is, public statements, force posture, and nuclear targeting. The clear aspects which he empirically proved is that the US decision makers did not articulate the policy to use nuclear weapons for the purpose of limited nuclear war because such policy was unpopular with the public. Alternatively, state officials publicized nuclear deterrence policy based on the so called MAD policy.
2. Mitchell Waldrop, Complexity: The Emerging Science at the Edge of Order and Chaos, Sterling Lord Literistic Inc. 1995. Also, see llya Prigogine, From Being to Becoming, (1984).; Gregorie Nocolis a llya Prigogine, Exploring Complexity, An Introduction (1987)
3. Richard Little and Michael Smith ed. Perspective on World Politics, 2nd ed. London and New York: Routledge (1991).
4. See my paper, "New Dimensions of Global Modeling" read at the 25th ISAGA held at University of Michigan (1995).
5. Hiroharu Seki, Influence of the Periphery on the Center in Global Modeling and Political Philosophy. Ritsumeikan Journal of IR and Area Studies, Vol. 3, (1992).
6. Ritsumeikan Journal of IR and Area Studies, No. 9, pp. 1-15 (1996).
7. John Lewis Gaddis, Nuclear Weapons and Cold War History, in "Nuclear Rivalry and International Order", (ed.) by Jorn Gjelstad and Olav Njolstad Sage Publications, (1996).

8. See Michael McKinley, "The Tragic Equivalence: Congruences in the Theories and Practices of Economics and War" presented at 37th ISA Convention in San Diego, (1996).
9. Later development of new idea for university network came from the activity of the UNU in this critical period. Hiroharu Seki, "New Stage of University Exchange Program as a Frontier of Alternative Approach to Global Development", Ritsumeikan Journal of IR and Area Studies, No. 5, pp. 99-109, (1993).
10. Prehistory for Roman Catholic Pope's visit to Japan by the effort of the UNU is roughly described in my book "The Asia Pacific in the Global Transformation, Bringing the Nation State Japan Back In," Institute of Oriental Culture, University of Tokyo, (1987); see Chapters 9, 10, 11 in this book. The Pope declared from Nagasaki that the use of nuclear weapons in the war imposes threat to the human survival and it should be defined as the evil war as well as the crime to the human being. Therefore the Pope clearly conclude that "the responsibilities of scientists and engineers are very significant for this situation" because 60 per cent of scientists or engineers are working in the military related industries particularly in the US and in the USSR for innovating weapons technology. Later in 1982, Chicago Catholic Church started to prepared the Pastoral letter to declare the nuclear war as the crime to the God. It was publicized finally in May, 1983. In this, the Pastoral Letter also explained the reason of the nuclear war as the crime by clearly pointing that such war could not be characterized as just war irrespective of the situation. It also severely criticized nuclear deterrence as a preparation of the crime.
11. *Ibid.*
12. Eric Mlyn, *op. cit.*, and Jorn Gjelstad and Olav Njorstad, *op. cit.*
13. See my paper, Potential Capabilities of CSCE Process for the Application to the CSCA Process, paper read at Vienna Joint Symposium between American University and Ritsumeikan University organized by Frances Mautner-Markhov.
14. See my paper read at the 37th ISA San Diego Convention, "The Meaning of the Sea of Japan (Tong Hai) Rim in the Post Cold War Periods, Creating the Alternative Global Transformation Process in the Asia Pacific Region" (1996).
15. Imre Lakatos and Alan Musgrave (eds.), Criticism and the Growth of Knowledge, (1972).

4

Use of Chemical and Biological Weapons Against Vietnam in 1973

Toxic substances have been employed as a method of warfare for ages although their use has continuously been condemned. First efforts to formally ban these weapons are reflected in the Brussels Declaration of 1874 and the Hague Conventions of 1899 and 1907.[1] Those international agreements notwithstanding, chemical warfare on a large scale occurred during the First World War. It resulted in approximately 1.3 million casualties, 100,000 of them fatal.

Increasing public awareness of the horrors of chemical warfare stimulated further efforts aimed at a ban on CW. The Treaty of Versailles prohibited Germany, the state which had used chemical weapons first in World War I, from manufacturing or importing poisonous gases.[2] Other peace treaties of 1919-20 contained similar provisions.[3] The treaty of Washington which was to limit the use of submarines but never entered into force, included limitations on the use of noxious gases.[4]

A clause similar to the one used for the treaty of Washington was included in the Convention Limiting Arms in Central America (signed in 1923).[5]

Efforts to prohibit chemical warfare were intensified with the creation of the League of Nations. A number of committees were established to consider various aspects of a CW ban, including the possibility of prohibiting laboratory experiments in this field and requiring states to make scientific discoveries. It was proposed to undertake a study on the effects of chemical and bacteriological welfare to educate and raise public attention to this issue.

The Geneva Protocol

In May 1925, a conference on methods to control the international arms trade was convened in Geneva within the framework of the League of Nations. At this conference, the United States initially proposed a prohibition of the export of chemical weapons. Many states objected to such a ban because it was deemed discriminatory, favouring the States which already possessed chemical weapons or had the means and know-how to produce them. It was also said that export controls in this field were difficult if not impossible to implement. And finally, it was argued that such an obligation would not necessarily prevent the use of CW in future wars. On the other hand, a technical committee of the Conference reached the conclusion that a prohibition of the production of CW, which was put forward as an alternative, was not accepted by many countries.

The United States, therefore, proposed to conclude an agreement banning the use of chemical weapons in war. As a result of a Polish initiative, biological means of warfare were added to it. On 17 June 1925, the Protocol for the Prohibition of the Use in War of Asphyxiating, Poisonous or Other Gases, and of Bacteriological Methods of Warfare was adopted.[6] It was, by and large, modelled after Article 5 of the Washington Treaty of 1922. Until today, the majority of States, 121 as of end July 1989,[7] have become parties to the Geneva Protocol. The UN General Assembly has, repeatedly and in resolution adopted by consensus, called upon all States, including States not parties to the Protocol, to abide strictly by its principles and objectives.[8] This has led the majority of States to assume that the obligations expressed in the Geneva Protocol have become part of customary international law which means that parties as well as non-parties are bound by its provisions.

In addition to the limited scope of the Protocol, one of its weak points is that some 40 States have expressed reservations when ratifying or acceding to it. These reservations permit the States concerned to use chemical weapons to retaliate in-kind if they were attacked by such means. This has resulted in a situation where most States consider the Geneva Protocol a non first-use regime. Another reservation which has been expressed by some States, confines the application of the agreement to other parties. This would allow the use of CW against non-parties. Although this second type of reservation has not been withdrawn by the countries concerned, there is a clear tendency to consider the Protocol applicable to non-parties as well, particularly since the agreement is viewed by most States as part of customary international law. Occasionally, it has been argued that the Protocol only applies to international wars (the Protocol bans the use of CW in war), and that the internal use of CW is not prohibited. The predominant opinion of States and private legal experts, however, does not support this view.

The Disarmament Conference of the League of Nations

As a consequence of the obvious limits of the Geneva Protocol, efforts for a total ban on chemical weapons continued within the framework of the League of Nations. At the League's Disarmament Conference in 1932-33, several proposals for chemical and biological disarmament were put forward. Many of them contained provisions on the prevention of development and production of chemical and biological weapons in peacetime, and the destruction of existing stockpiles. A special committee of the conference was established to deal with these questions. It considered a broad variety of issues, including the definition of chemical and biological weapons, the monitoring of compliance with a ban, and sanctions to be applied in case of violations. A draft disarmament convention submitted by Britain in March 1933 reflected a number of these considerations. It provided for the prohibition of use of chemical and biological weapons in war, also with regard to non-parties to the treaty. It permitted the use of CW for retaliatory purposes, but unconditionally banned the use of biological weapons. It also stated that chemical and biological weapons must not be developed at any time. The definition of CW used in the British draft was comprehensive, including tear gas and incendiary devices.

Having reached no concrete result, the Disarmament Conference recessed in January 1936 and failed to reconvene due to rising tensions in Europe and the outbreak of the Second World War in 1939. It resulted, however, in a thorough consideration of many important aspects related to chemical and biological disarmament, and some questions discussed are still relevant in today's negotiations on the projected CWC.[9]

World War II and After

During the inter-war period and the Second World War two major violations of the Geneva Protocol occurred. Italy, a party to the Geneva

Protocol since 1928, used chemical weapons from 1935 to 1936 in its war against Abyssinia. It first denied the allegations but then justified the use of chemical weapons by saying that it was permitted as a reprisal against other illegal acts of war, an argument which was questionable from a legal point of view.

Mainly tear and mustard gas were employed (dropped from aeroplanes) to protect the flanks of advancing columns, to disrupt the enemy's communication and to demoralize its troops. Opinion is divided over the military effectiveness of these actions. However, some sources reported up to 15,000 casualties resulting from the use of chemical weapons. Other violations of the Geneva Protocol probably took place from 1937 to 1945. Japan reportedly used CW in its war against China: A wide range of chemicals, including tear gas, phosgene, hydrogen cyanide, mustard gas and other agents were used against troops as well as the civilians, resulting in several thousand casualties.

When the Second World War broke out, only modest CW stockpiles existed. These stocks were gradually increased during the war, but they were not used on a significant scale. This is often attributed to the fact that most of the big powers had chemical weapons in their arsenals and, as a result, there was a situation of mutual deterrence, in-kind. The second factor often mentioned is that there were military concerns over the value of chemical weapons.[10] Indeed, the military value of chemical weapons remains even today a subject of controversy and the opinion of the military is divided. The debate over whether chemical weapons are the poor man's nuclear bomb is an example. Another factor said to have prevented recourse to chemical warfare during World War II was the impact of the Geneva Protocol, the international legal norm which existed against the use of CW.

During and after World War II, the major powers accumulated large arsenals of chemical weapons and development of ever more poisonous chemical warfare agents continued unabated. Some countries, however, disposed of their stockpiles after the war.[11] Nerve agents were discovered during World War II [12] and the V. Agents, another type of nerve agent during the mid-1950s. Nerve agents interfere with or inhibit the transmission of nerve impulses by disrupting the enzymatic reactions in the nervous system. They are often referred to as second generation chemical weapons. Their lethality is many times higher than that of agents used during the First World War. The manufacturing of incapacitating agents such as BX was standardized by the early 1960s. Incapacitating agents are chemicals which cause temporary disease or induce temporary mental or physical disability, the duration of which extends far past the period of exposure. They are designed to reduce the combat effectiveness of enemy forces. Renewed interest in chemical weapons on the part of the military was reflected in this situation and was also responsible for the development of new means of deployment of chemical warfare agents.[13]

Renewed Attention to the Problem of Chemical and Biological Weapons and United Nations' Involvement

Developments in the CW domain went largely unnoticed by the public worldwide due to the rising focus on nuclear weapons. Chemical and biological weapons were classified as weapons of mass destruction by the United Nations Commission for Conventional Armaments in 1948,[14] but the discussions in international fora, including the United Nations, during the 1950s and first half of thc 1960s remained inconclusive. Proposals for general and complete disarmament put forward at this time included provisions on chemical weapons, but were never seriously examined. Two major allegations of the use of CW were made during that period. China and a number of NGOs accused the United States of using chemical weapons in the Korean war from 1951 to 1952. However, no independent confirmation of the allegations was produced. There were many reports that Egyptian armed forces had used chemical weapons from 1963 to 1967 during their intervention in the Yemeni civil war. No conclusive and independent confirmation was published. But the evidence produced by various States and NGOs was considered more substantial than in the Korean case.

In October 1954, the Federal Republic of Germany foreswore the right to produce or strockpile on its territory chemical and biological weapons (and nuclear ones as well)[15]. This was a prerequisite for joining the Western European Union (WEU), and later North Atlantic Treaty Organization (NATO). Under this agreement, the Federal Republic of Germany accepted international verification measures including on-site inspections, a unique obligation at that time. These controls on West-German chemical and biological armament have been effective since 1956 and are performed by the WEU Armaments Control Agency.

It was that use of chemicals on a large scale by the United States in the Second Indo-China war which, again brought the question of chemical warfare to the attention of the public and placed it on the international arms control agenda. In the early 1960s the United States began to use gradually increasing qualities of herbicides and defoliants agents,[16] for war purposes in Indochina. These chemicals were employed to deprive enemy forces of cover by defoliating the vegetation, and to destroy crops. The use of herbicides was stopped in 1970/71. Considerable quantities of irritant agents, mainly the tear gas CS, were used during various military operations such as the so-called tunnel or bunker-warfare, or rescue missions. Irritant agents are short-term incapacitants used to cause rapid disablement that lasts little longer than the time of exposure.

The United States and Australia argued that the substances employed in Indochina were not chemical weapons and that their use in armed conflict was therefore not prohibited by the Geneva Protocol. (The United States did not join the Protocol until 1975). However, these activities were perceived by many States as chemical warfare. A resolution by the UN General Assembly which included herbicides in its definition of CW was passed in 1969 by a significant majority of votes in favour.

Another reaction to the use of chemical in the Indochina war was a UN General Assembly resolution, originally proposed by Hungary. It was adapted in 1966. It called for the strict observance of the Geneva Protocol, and invited all States to ratify or accede to the Protocol.[17] The resolution however, stopped short of condemning the United States.[18]

Agony of the Vietnamese: Second Indochina War

The most massive chemical warfare in history was that waged by the US military against Indochina, almost coinciding with the American CBW bicentennial. Even after a lapse of more than twenty-seven years the people of Indochina are courageously facing the long term effects of chemicals, especially those due to Agent Orange on land, crops, forest vegetation, livestock, and human beings. Ironically, many of the US army personnel who were exposed to the chemicals in course of military operations are also suffering from similar maladies. The Indochina chemical warfare is that saga of untold miseries which have been caused by the cruellest and the maddest and the most shameful attack perpetrated by man on man and nature. The story is now known in some detail, but many a mystery is yet to be unfolded. It has many ramifications and implications and has assumed global significance.

On the recommendation of the then Secretary of State, President Kennedy approved the use of chemical defoliants, after having been convinced that defoliants are the only means to subdue a guerrilla army sheltered by forest cover. In the process crops were also destroyed, thereby starving to death daily 4,000 soldiers for every acre of land sprayed with chemicals. It turned out to be that the operation was not simply one of defoliation and crop destruction. The amounts sprayed were many times more than what were needed for defoliation. The effect was unbelievably harmful. Moreover, diozin which was present in variable quantities as a highly toxic contaminant came along with the herbicides and defoliants. In fact, diozin had added a new dimension to the Indochina chemical warfare, the story of which, very likely, is going to be told in terms of dioxin–its high concentration, whether accidental or deliberate and its harmful and long-term effects on man in the form of blindness, liver damage, cancer, miscarriage, birth defects, genetic abnormalities, etc., and on nature in the form of loss of forest trees, crops, aquatic life mainly fisheries, soil fertility, etc. The tragedy is that while some well-meaning people are engaged in disentangling the complicated cobweb of the dioxin story and finding remedial measures against its toxic effects, another group of the same species is assiduously engaged in producing more toxic chemicals and developing more sophisticated techniques to kill their kins, after calling them foes for this purpose. We will come to this aspect in the subsequent chapter of this study.

The US army used several chemicals including Agents Orange, White and Blue during the Vietnam war. The nature of all these chemicals and their short and long-term effects are quite exhaustively documented by Vietnamese and other scientists against the Vietnamese scenario (Chemical Warfare, Vietnamese Studies No. 29). The global awareness has taken several years to come. If any single person whose crusading efforts could be said to have aroused this awareness it was Prof. Ton That Tung, the world famous liver surgery expert of Vietnam. His own studies on the long-term carcinogenic and teratogenic effects of herbicides on man convinced beyond doubt many a dissident and brought them rounds to his point of view.

About the Chemicals: Dioxin Content

The three major chemical agents employed by the US army in the operation referred to as Ranch Hand were:

1. Agent Orange – a mixture, in varying proportions, of 2, 4-D (2,4-Dichlorophenoxyacetic acid) and 2,4,5–T (2,4,5–Trichlorophenoxyacetic acid) in the form of either salts or esters, and small but unknown quantities of TCDD or simply dioxin (2, 3, 7, 8–Tetrachlorodibenzo- P-dioxin). The last one is a highly toxic substance and is invariably a contaminant of 2, 4, 5–T.

2. Agent White is a mixture of 2, 4–D and picloram (4–amino 3, 4, 6-Trichloropicolinic acid).

3. Agent Blue is the sodium salt of dimethylarsenic or cacodylinc acid. Orange, White and Blue are the colours of the labels of containers and have nothing to do with the colour of the agents themselves.

Agent Orange was used to destroy mainly forests and Agent Blue to destroy cultivated crops. Of the total quantity of these Agents amounting to 72 million litres according to official US figures, Agent Orange accounted for 61 per cent, Agent white 29 per cent and Agent Blue 11 per cent. The major thrust was thus directed to the destruction of forests. In fact, according to the Vietnamese estimates 44 per cent of forests and 43 per cent of crop lands were destroyed. The US estimates are respectively 12 per cent and 5 per cent affected by dioxin.

The contention about the concentration of dioxin in Agent Orange has not been resolved. It is only the US army which can provide the actual figures. They are unknown. The US veterans estimate that the total amount of dioxin was not less than 170 kilogram. The Vietnamese scientists estimate that the dosage of Agent Orange varied considerably and hence the amounts of dioxin sprayed with it also varied, say, between 25–30 kilograms and 200–300 kilograms. Academician Fokin is of the view that according to available information the total amount of dioxin sprayed was about 500 kilograms. It may be pointed out that if sprayed uniformly, this quantity of dioxin would have been enough to kill or maim or incapacitate in one form or the other the bulk of the world's population.

Either as herbicide or as defoliant or as crop-destroyer, only very small amounts of these chemicals are required but the US army sprayed repeatedly high concentrations in the same area, to ensure that the destruction is complete.

Insult to Ecosystem

The longest and the most drastic insult to ecosystem ever perpetrated by man was perhaps that done by the US army in the Vietnam war. This was the result of the nearly 15 years of spray of chemicals, apparently herbicides and defoliants, beginning from 1961. The most massive use was launched in the mid to late sixties. The dosage was many times more than what would be required for herbicides and defoliants. In many ways the chemical war waged on Vietnam was unique, in duration, in land area covered both in the forest and crop occupied zones, and the intensity of attack. The effect of the chemicals was not limited directly to the vegetational cover, as one would understand from the use of the terms herbicides and defoliants, but spread out on human beings, animals and other flora and fauna. On land as well as the equatic regions. All such toxic chemicals are meant to be used in very low doses, so that no toxicity, in an ideal case, is caused to any object other than the target. In general such ideality is not the rule, but the toxicity caused to other objects is kept at a minimum, so that nature can recover from the insult within a reasonably short period. If the dosage is just above the limit, the effects may be of many kinds and complicated too. The ecosystem is not only insulted, if gets a shock and nature does not have the experience to recover. In fact, every component of an ecosystem in continually producing rather small disturbances in nature which are actually necessary for its survival. Nature means that way, and is capable of withstanding that change and of bringing, as quickly as possible, the ecosystem to a balanced state. The shock to the ecosystem of Vietnam was of such severity that even after 15-20 years nature has not been able to recover from it. There is no knowing whether the attackers were already aware of the consequences of such intensive use of chemicals through small scale studies or laboratory experiments or not, but it appears that some of the veterans were themselves shocked both ecologically and emotionally. The shock may be comparable with the first sight of the holocaust produced by the atomic bombs dropped during the Japanese war.

The long term effects of chemical warfare on man and nature so far revealed from the studies of the Vietnamese scientists and those of veterans and scientists of other countries have thrown up a long list of complex problems. In fact, much of what has happened and is likely to happen, is still shrouded in many uncertainties and doubts.

Damage to Plant and Forest Ecology

In spite of the fact that a systematic and large-scale chemical war was waged on Vietnam, the US Defence Department reported that herbicides used in Vietnam had not caused serious damage to the ecology. Many other in US held contrary view. In fact the Midwest Research Institute in USA belonged to the latter category, and sent F.H. Tschirely to investigate. He confirmed serious effects on the flora wherever herbicides were used. Others who followed, particularly Dr. Pfeffer and his co-workers, were definitely of the view that the second Indochina war was an ecocide war. They published the results of their investigations in Science (1970). Twelve years later Prof. Arthur H. Westing noted: The result in South Vietnam was the widespread long-lasting and severe disruption of forest lands, of perennial croplands and of farmlands—that is to say of millions of hectares of the natural resource base essential to an agrarian society.

The total sprayed area constitutes, as already mentioned, nearly 44 per cent of cultivated land, 43 per cent of forest land, mostly belonging to South Vietnam and only a part of the territory of North Vietnam. The chemical war was taken beyond the boundaries of Vietnam into Laos and Kampuchea, which suffered similar consequences, although on a smaller scale.

The chemical war not only led to the destruction of the ecology of Vietnam but inflicted physical and psychological suffering which perhaps has no parallel in human history. Notwithstanding this agony the human will of the Vietnamese people could not be suppressed. After a prolonged and protracted war they succeeded in defending the independence and sovereignty of their country. This shows that human will and spirit are even today stronger than all weapons of mass destruction. It is this single biggest factor which created a new vibration among the people within the United States.

This is how this moved was reflected by one of the outstanding writers of the United States.

"Crisis after crisis these past twenty years had seemingly numbed us to crisis, emergency becoming in our time man's ordinary state. But Vietnam is no Berlin or Korea or Cuba. Vietnam siezes us in a new hold, fingers a new nerve, persuades us that this war is a most distinguished and fateful event. Of course, it has certain allies in this persuasion. American racial problems worsen even as our leaders try hardest to end them. Urban disaster deepens even as our leaders attack it head-on with their best available will and ingenuity. The militarization of our political economy accelerated even as our leaders find themselves most lonely in the grand defense of Western liberty. A new sectarianism turns us angrily against one another at home, and the West European states begin to individuate themselves within the alliance even as our leaders demand more unity, global and domestic. But the war alone would be ominous enough. No one pretends anymore to see its limits. Everyone is forced to admit that it seems to be opended an eternal war.

Men have died before now. Why should Vietnam disrupt Western composure so deeply? We have the same explanations for this war that we had for all the others. Why do these explanations now seem so banal and inappropriate, so unworthy of the moment? Why are so many Americans–so many more Europeans–not satisfied to hear that the liberal West has again gone forth on a new march of the old holy war against totalitarianism? Why are so many of us no longer rejuvenated by the old tales? It cannot be the hardships of the war that make the difference. Americans never having been afraid of the hardships of violence; nor the elusiveness of victory, Americans always having been ready to do what is needed to win what must be won.

The problem seems to be that we are no longer sure what victory means. The Western liberalism the formerly produced such convincing and useful definitions of victory and defeat presented with this war, stands mute.

Since the old truths refuse to function, since in neither Vietnam nor Mississippi do the old pleasure-pain remedies solve our problems, we begin to wonder in the back of our minds if they ever really solved anything before. Maybe they were only postponements or quarantines, these successes of the past. Maybe there now seems to be no more time for postponement, no more places of quarantine, no more excuses for not coming to a judgment.

This war is moving into our history in a unique way. It is not the first of its kind. But it is the first to be so big, so protracted, and above all so well observed: a whole nation beholds itself in the act–the act being (with whatever justice) the incineration of a whole other nation. Has any other culture ever possessed itself so openly–so carnally–as ours does now? We can scarcely return unchanged from this spectacle to dream the old dreams, take comfort in the old verities: we cannot worship again in the old church because we cannot now deny that there is blood on the altar, that the priests hands are not steady. With this war, history becomes the intimate affair of each one of us, a private act for which each of us has to account personally.

No culture has been more violent than has our Western culture. It was the West which framed the valutingly arrogant concept of the savage; the West which gave the horizon itself a distinctively political meaning, maintaining that what it could not yet see existed in order to be made visible to it at some future time, to be subject to it, civilized by it, or, if found to be an obstacle to its enlarging of the bounds of human empire, destroyed by it. There has been moment when the people of the West who have been customarily granted the reprieve of ignorance, have stood so specifically exposed to a clear view of their culture's capacities for violence. This essay on Vietnam is thus an essay on the West." [20]

This assessment by an American writer written almost three decades ago speaks for itself and needs no comment. The moral of this war against Vietnamese people is that it pricked the conscience of the common American people.

One is not born with a political commitment. One receives certain values, tries to apply them with honesty and as much skill as one can muster, and tries to have the courage to accept whatever personal commitments the results may imply. The pattern of argument in this study essentially follows the process by which one comes to be the particular sort of partisan that one is.

The effort is to probe the specific for the principle it embodies and the untrue for the truth it palliates; to move through the superficial platitudes about Vietnam towards firmer, more well-bodied generalizations about the cold war and the longer term conflict within the West and between the West and the East of which the cold war appeared to be the tragic episode of the contemporary world.

Thus the subsequent chapters of this study examines how biological and chemical weapons still haunt like a nightmare the people of our planet. The main purpose of the subsequent chapters is to reconstruct the argument that pious wishes are no substitute to the will of the people to hold back the hands of perpetrators of weapons of mass destruction.

REFERENCES

1. The Brussels Declaration prohibited the use of poisons and poisoned bullets in war. The Hague Conventions did the same and a separate declaration (IV. 2 of 29 July, 1899) or the Hague Conference banned the use of projectiles the sole object which was the diffusion of asphyxiating or deleterious gases.
2. Treaty of Peace with Germany, Versailles, 28 June, 1919, Art. 171.
3. Treaty of Saint Germain, Art. 135, Treaty of Neuilly, Art. 82, Treaty of Trianon, Art. 119, Treaty of Servers, Art. 176.
4. Treaty of Washington, 6.2.1922, in particular Article V. Britain, France, Italy, Japan and the United States were involved in the negotiations. The treaty stated that the use of gas in war was prohibited under international law.
5. Convention for the Limitation of Armaments of Central American States, 7.2.1923, Article V.
6. It prohibits the use in war of asphyxiating, poisonous or other gases, and of all analogous liquids, materials or devices and the use of bacteriological methods of warfare.
7. Information received from the Depository of the Protocol for a List of the Parties see, for example, the UN Disarmament Yearbook.
8. E.g. A/43/74.
9. A detailed description of the proposals can be found in SIPRI, Problems of Chemical and Biological Warfare, Vol. IV, Stockholm and New York 1971.
10. Concerns at the top military level in Germany that the use of CW might inhibit the rapid movement of troops is an example.
11. The United Kingdom had destroyed its CW stockpiles by 1956. Also, Canada reported that it had destroyed its CW (CCD/434, CD/173). Many experts believe that France has retained at least parts of its stockpile although the situation in this case is not entirely clear.
12. Their discovery originates in German organo-phosphate pesticide research during the Second World War. Nerve agents include, inter alia, Tabun, Sarin and Soman. Another nerve agent, VX was discovered in the United Kingdom after the war.
13. E.g., multiple rocket launchers, clustered bomblets, and surface-to-surface missiles at a later stage.
14. The Commission for Conventional Armaments was a subsidiary body of the UN Security Council and functioned from 1947 to 1950. A resolution of the UN General Assembly, adopted on 24 January 1946, demanded the elimination of atomic weapons and of all other major weapons adaptable to mass destruction.
15. Declaration by the Federal Chancellor, in Annexure No. 1 to the 19 Protocol no. 3 on the control of armaments to the 1954.
16. The chemicals used were Agent Orange, a substance which had several unintended effects because it was contaminated with super-toxic impurity and agents Blue and White.

17. A/2162 B (XXI).
18. Courtesy: UNIDIR (United Nations Institute for Disarmament Research).
19. Dr. Sushil Kumar Mukharjee : The Indochina Reports pp. 50-56, : 1984.
20. Carl Oglesby and Richard Shaull, Containment and Change : 1982, pp. 3-5.

5

Use of Chemical and Biological Weapons in the gulf war and its Impact on the U.S. Armed Forces

In retrospect when one looks at the developments of the 20th century and that too in the last two years of this century, one cannot but come to the agonising conclusion that this century, notwithstanding its various achievements in the area of economic developments, science and technology, and massive use of science and technology for the welfare of the people, it had an ugly side.

Gulf War Syndrome

It is in this century that weapons of mass destruction—were not only invented, their stockpiles built but also used to destroy million and millions of people. The mad race to fabricate weapons of mass destruction has not ended yet. In fact, this race is still on.

"History, constructed on concrete facts and mythology, records the use of chemical weapons on a number of occasions. It however, does not miss to capture the efforts made to stem such a use. The present century, in many ways, witnessed a flurry of activities revolving around chemical weapons. The comprehensive and voluminous application of this category of weapons in World War I led to much hue and cry. It resulted in the conclusion of the Geneva Protocol. Similarly, the American use of chemical weapons in the Indochina struggle pressurized the world to take a few more steps to address the menace of this class of weapons. Nevertheless world public opinion kept struggling against the obstinacy and resistance of the US till the Gulf War. It was only when Saddam

Hussein's Iraq made the US realize the threat of chemical weapons proliferation in a more direct way, that the American decision makers began serious moves towards arriving at an international agreement to ban the use, production and possession of chemical weapons. Needless to mention the US Administration was convinced that the American nuclear weapon possession would not allow an adverse impact on its strategic superiority, even after the renunciation of the chemical option.''[1] There is something more to it than meets the eye.

Before we examine the various dimensions of proliferation and large scale use of biological and chemical weapons after Second World War, it will be relevant to mention how these weapons boomeranged on the American people themselves physically, morally, and spiritually. In the earlier chapter we have mentioned how the soul of the peace-loving American people was stirred by indiscriminate use of chemical weapons on the Vietnamese people. Let us now look at this problem from another angle. How biological and chemical weapons had serious implications for the American armed forces and their kith and kins.

In October 1992, the Committee on Banking, Housing and Urban Affairs, which has Senate oversight responsibility for the Export Administration Act (EAA), held an inquiry into the US export policy to Iraq prior to be Persian Gulf War. During that hearing it was learned that UN inspectors identified many US manufactured items exported pursuant to licenses issued by the US Department of Commerce that were used to further Iraq's chemical and nuclear weapons development and missile delivery system development programs.

On 30 June 1993, several veterans testified at a hearing of the Senate Committee on Armed Services. There they related details of unexplained events that took place during the Persian Gulf War which they believed to be chemical warfare agent attacks. After these unexplained events, many of the veterans present reported symptoms consistent with exposure to a mixed agent attack. Then on 29 July 1993, the Czech Minister of Defence announced that a Czechoslovak chemical decontamination unit had detected the chemical warfare agent Sarin in areas of northern Saudi Arabia during the early phases of the Gulf War. They had attributed the detections to fallout from coalition bombing of Iraqi chemical warfare agent production facilities.

In August 1993, Senate Banking Committee Chairman Donald W Reigle Jr. began to research the possibility of a connection between the

Iraqi chemical, biological, and radiological warfare research and development programs and a mysterious illness which was then being reported by thousands of returning Gulf War veterans. In September 1993, Senator Reigle released a staff report on this issue and introduced an amendment to the Fiscal Year 1994 National Defence Authorization Act that provided preliminary funds for research of the illnesses and investigation of reported exposures.

When this first staff report was released by Senator Riegle the estimate of the number of veterans suffering from these unexplained illnesses varied from hundreds, according to the Department of Defence to thousands according to the Department of Veterans Affairs. It is now believed that tens of thousands US Gulf veteran are suffering from a myriad of symptoms collectively labelled either as Gulf War Syndrome or Persian Gulf Syndrome or Desert War Syndrome. Hundreds and possibly thousands of servicemen and women who still are on active duty are reluctant to come forward for fear of losing their jobs and medical care. These Gulf War veterans are reporting muscle and joint pain, memory loss, intestinal and heart problems, fatigue, nasal congestions, urinary urgency, diarrhea, twitching, rashes, sores, and a number of other symptoms.

They began experiencing these multiple symptoms during and after—often many months after—their tour of duty in the Gulf. A number of the veterans who initially exhibited these symptoms have died since returning from the Gulf. Perhaps most disturbingly, members of the veteran's families are now suffering from these symptoms to a debilitating degree. The scope and urgency of this crisis demands an appropriate response.

This investigation into Gulf War Syndrome, which was initiated by the Banking Committee under the direction of Chairman Riegle has uncovered a large body of evidence linking the symptoms of the Syndrome to the exposure of Gulf War participants to chemical and biological warfare agents, chemical and biological warfare pre-treatment drugs, and other hazardous materials and substances. Since the release of the first staff report on 9 September, 1993, the inquiry has continued. Thousands of government officials, scientists and veterans have been interviewed or consulted, and additional evidence has been compiled.

Since the Banking Committee began its inquiry, the position of the Department of Defence regarding the possible causes of Gulf War

Syndrome was altered only when challenged with evidence that is difficult to dispute. Yet, despite the vast resources of the Department of Defence several independent and congressional inquires with limited resources continue to uncover additional evidence of hazardous exposures and suspicious events.

The Department of Defence, when first approached regarding this issue by the Committee staff, contended that there was no evidence that US forces were exposed to chemical warfare agents. However, during a telephone interview 7 September 1993 with Walter Reed Army Medical Center commander Major General Ronald Blanck, the Committee staff was informed that the issue of chemical and biological warfare agent exposure had not been explored because it was the position of "military intelligence" that such exposures never occurred.

Then, during 10 November 1993 press briefing at the Pentagon, the Department of Defence acknowledged that the Czech government did defect chemical agents in the Southwest Asia theatre of operations. After analyzing the results of the Czech report, the Department of Defence concluded that the defections were unrelated to the mysterious health problems that have victimized some of our veterans. According to former Secretary of Defence Les Aspin, in some cases the wind was wrong and the distances too great to suggest a link. For instance, Seabees serving to the south and east of the defection site have complained of persistent health problems; but according to the Pentagon, the wind was blowing in the other direction at the time of the defections and the concentrations were too low to cause harm over that kind of a distance.

The fact is, no one has ever suggested that there was a link between the Czech detections and what occurred during the early morning hours of 19 January 1991 near the Port of Jubayl. Former Defence Secretary Aspin said at the briefing that this incident could not have been from the Coalition bombings of the Iraqi chemical weapons facilities because the winds were blowing to the northwest. Yet according to available Soviet documents, the dispersal of chemical agents and other hazardous substances is controlled by other factors in addition to surface wind direction and velocity, such as topography, temperature, precipitation, vertical temperature gradient, and atmospheric humidity. These factors all contribute to the size and type of dispersal that will be observed. [2] Unclassified visual and thermal satellite imagery confirms that the fallout from the bombings of Iraqi targets during the air and ground war moved to the southeast, with the weather patterns and upper atmospheric wind currents, towards coalition force positions.

According to a knowledgeable source who has requested confidentiality, the Czechs believed that the detections were caused by the weather inversion which occurred that day (January 19, 1991) as the weather front moved southward. The Czechoslovak chemical detection unit reported this information to US command officials immediately, but the responding units were unable to confirm their findings when they arrived, according to the Pentagon. Nonetheless, at the November 10, 1993 briefing, the Department of Defence admitted that the Czech detection were believed to be valid. The Department of Defence failed to disclose that the Czechoslovak chemical detection team also detected yperite that morning. The presence of both of these agents in such close proximity could only reasonably be the result of one of two possibilities: (1) direct Iraqi mixed agent attack, or (2) fallout from the coalition bombings of Iraqi weapons facilities and storage bunkers.

Defence Department officials, having had possession of the Czech report for over a month, were at a loss to explain the chemical mustard agent detected by the Czechoslovak chemical detection team in the Saudi desert near Kind Khalid Military City on January 24, 1991. This despite the fact that both the Czechs and French claim that this detection was reported to US command authorities during the Persian Gulf War.[3] Additionally, during the Gulf War, the Czechs claimed that they detected chemical nerve agent after a Scud missile attack. These statements, herctofore only reported in the press, have been confirmed by a member of the US Ist Cavalry Division and by an entire platoon of a US Army chemical detection unit who trained with the Czechoslovak chemical detection unit near King Khalid Military City.

The contents of this report supports the conclusion that US forces were exposed to some level of chemical and possibly biological warfare agents during their service in the Gulf War. Any review conducted by the Pentagon must extend far beyond the information being reported by the Czech Ministry of Defence. The Czech information, while important represents just a small fraction of the evidence currently available.

It is now the position of the Department of Defence that it has no other evidence that US forces were exposed to chemical agents. Yet direct eyewitness accounts provide evidence which suggests that gas was detected, along with many other events which may have been actual attacks on US forces.

This shows that the US forces were exposed also to chemical agents. The assertion that the levels of nerve agent detected by the Czechs and others were not harmful is flawed. In subsequent requirements for chemical detection equipment, the Department of the Army acknowledges that the principal chemical agent detection alarm deployed during the war, the M8A1 was not sufficiently sensitive to detect sustained low levels of chemical agent and to monitor personnel for contamination.[4] Further, US Army Material Safety Data Sheets indicate that chronic exposures to levels of over 0.0001 mg/m^3 of Sarin is hazardous and requires the use of protective equipment. The minimum level of chemical agent required to activate the automatic chemical agent detection alarm M8A1 commonly in use during the war exceeds this threshold by a factor of 1,000[5].

"The findings of this report prepared at the request of Chairman Reigle detail many other events reported by US servicemen and women that in some cases confirm the detection of chemical agents by US forces. In other cases these reports indicate the need for further detailed investigation. But still the question remains: Is exposure to these and other chemical agents the cause of Gulf War Syndrome? We have received hundreds of reports that many of these symptoms are being experienced by family members. Numerous developments have taken place over the last several months which suggest that, while chemical agents and other environmental hazards may have contributed to the Gulf War illnesses, bacteriological, fungal, and possibly other biological illnesses may be the fundamental cause. This position is supported by the following."

"First Dr. Edward S. Hyman, a New Orleans bacteriologist, has treated a small number of the sick veterans and several of their wives for bacteriological infections, and has developed a protocol of treatment that has resulted in symptom abatement in many of his patients.

"Second, during the November 10, 1993 unclassified briefing for Members of the US Senate, in response to direct questioning, then Under Secretary of Defence John Deutch said that the Department of Defence was withholding classified information on the exposure of US forces to biological materials. In a Department of Defence-sponsored conference on counter-proliferation held at Los Alamos National Laboratory on 6-7 May, 1994. Dr. Deutch admitted that biological agent detection is a priority development area for the Department of Defence since there currently is no biological agent detection system fielded with any US forces anywhere in the world."

"Third the Department of Defence has named Dr. Joshua Lederberg to head its research team into the causes of Gulf War illnesses. Dr. Lederberg among his other credits, is a Nobel Laureate and an expert in the fields of bacteriology genetics, and biological warfare defences."

First hand accounts and other documentary evidence including reports in the print media confirm that "the Department of Defence assertions are inaccurate. We believe there is reliable evidence that US forces were exposed to chemical and possibly biological agents." It goes on to underline that "regardless of whether US forces were exposed or not, the entire official body of information including all classified or heretofore unpublished information, available research data sets, case histories, and diagnostic breakdown information must be made available to independent civilian medical researchers in order to further the research into the causes of and treatments for these illnesses. Absent a release of information by the Department of Defence of the science which forms the bases for their theories the Department of Defence position must be viewed by qualified scientists as anecdotal and unsubstantiated."

"Given that there is also a growing body of evidence indicating that spouses and children of Gulf War veterans are vulnerable to similar illnesses the Department of Defence must now share all of its information with civilian non-governmental researchers. These family members are civilians who may be at risk. This illness was first reported over three years ago."

"On February 9, 1994, Chairman Riegle sent a letter to Secretary of Defence William Perry asking that he release all US military personnel from any oath of secrecy they may have taken regarding classified information specifically pertaining to chemical or biological warfare agent exposure in the Persian Gulf theatre. This request was based on a recommendation of the National Academy of Sciences, National Institute of Medicine in their 1993 publication, *Veterans at Risk: The Health Effects of Mustard Gas and Lewistite*. On May 4, 1994, the Secretaries of Defence, Health and Human Services, and Veterans Affairs responded to the Chairman's letter stating that there was no classified information on chemical or biological detections or exposures. This directly contradicts the statement of Deputy Secretary Deutch in his November 10, 1993 unclassified briefing to Members and Staff."[6]

Nevertheless, the harsh reality is that affilicted American veterans are sick and suffering and some have died. Others are now destitutes having spent tens of thousands of dollars, depleting their life savings in an unsuccessful search for an explanation for their ailments. This in itself is a telling indictment of weapons of mass destruction, particularly of those who fabricate them and use them against other nations.

This is not the place to discuss how Iraq possessed a large and sophisticated chemical and biological weapons production complex and which are the forces which helped it in this process. What needs to be highlighted is the consequences of chemical and biological weapons, direct and indirect on lives of people, both armed forces and the civilians. The devastation caused from the short term and long term point of view needs to be objectively assessed.

There is a growing body of evidence, which supports the claims of Gulf War American veterans that exposure to chemical and biological warfare agents may be the cause of the illnesses they currently suffer. There appear to be four primary sources of exposure: (1) as a result of direct attack via missile, rocket, artillery, or aircraft ammunitions, (2) as a result of intermittent low-level exposure to fallout from coalition bombing of Iraqi chemical and biological warfare plants and munitions bunkers, (3) as a result of administration of a nerve agent pre-treatment drug that acts in a manner similar to actual nerve agent, and (4) as a result of continuing contact with the Iraqi enemy prisoners of war.

In addition, there appear to be two secondary sources of exposure (1) exposure to occupation/environmental hazards in South West Asia and to contaminated material returned from the theatre of operations, and (2) transmission among family members' exposure to endemic diseases and illness. Hundreds of Gulf War veterans have been interviewed and they have confirmed what is called "Gulf War Syndrome".

Direct Exposure Events

Units located in areas where missile and rocket attack of aerial explosions occurred are reporting high rates of illnesses. The areas in which these events occurred were key logistic and staging areas, as well as those areas which were breached during the liberation of Kuwait.

Many veterans of these units have reported seeing large numbers of dead or dying animals in the area after the attacks; one veteran noted that all the insects were dead too.

Let us examine some specific reported cases, which became victims of chemical and biological weapons during the Gulf War. According to one non-commissioned officer in charge of arms and ammunitions shipments on 17 January 1991 he heard a loud explosion, which was followed by a sounding of alarms. As he was running to the bunker, his face began to burn. One member of the unit just dropped. About ten minutes later, according to him, the unit's first sergeant came by and told members of the unit to go to the highest level of alert. The unit remained at that level for 24 hours.

Two or three days later, he began feeling ill and noticed blood in his urine. Several other members of the unit began experiencing problems with their rectums. Of the unit's 110 soldiers, 85 now suffer from medical problems, and one, Staff Sergeant, who he described as having been in good physical shape, has inexplicably died. He described another member of the unit, Staff Sergeant as being seriously incapacitated.

He, a former teacher and Vietnam veteran, carries a notebook with him everywhere. He claims to have a severe problem with memory loss. He quit his job because he kept passing out and getting lost on the way to work. Other symptoms being suffered by him include headaches, blood in his urine, insomnia, joint and muscle pain, deteriorating vision, loss of mobility in his left arm, night sweats, and diaorrhea, sometimes bloody.

Another officer said that between 2.00 a.m. and 3.00 a.m. on January 20, 1991, there was a real bad explosion overhead. The alarms went off and everybody started running towards their bunkers. This officer said that there was a sharp odour of ammonia in the air. His eyes burned and his skin stung. His unit donned full chemical gear for nearly two hours until the all clear was given.[7] This officer says he has since experienced fatigue, sore joints, running nose, a chronic severe rash, and open sores which have been diagnosed as an itching problem.

Yet another official complained that since returning home from the Gulf, he has suffered a severe thyroid problem, a heart attack, memory loss, tired and aching joints, rashes on his feet, nervousness, and muscle cramps, although he reported no bleeding. He has had about ten blood tests and two sets of X-rays performed at the medical centre.

What is surprising that in February 1992, his daughter began developing a thyroid problem and has been suffering from nervousness, headaches, and fatigue. Over the last year, his wife has begun to develop these symptoms as well. There is no history of thyroid problems in family.

In an another case, an official in the summer of 1991, began feeling tired and having headaches. He consulted a private doctor, who said he was probably working too hard in the sun. He says he does not think he is as ill as the rest of the men in his unit. He feels that he has levelled out, but he still has good and bad days. He currently suffers from fatigue, headaches, weight gain, itching, muscle and joint pains, and memory loss.

His wife is also ill, he feels that she is more ill than he is. She has an enlarged spleen, an enlarged liver and abnormal liver functions, joint pains, night sweats, fatigue, stomach problems, itching, and rashes, but has not complained of memory loss. Two of his children are also complaining of headaches, joint and abdominal pains. His 13-year-old daughter was diagnosed as having mononucleosis. She also has sinus infections, and throat pains from the sinus drainage. His 11-year old son has had rashes, headaches, joint pain, itching, sinus and throat infections, and fevers.

One can go on giving details of the suffering of victims of biological and chemical weapons in the Gulf War on the basis of official and press reports. This entire evidence leads to one conclusion that not only direct victims of these weapons, their relatives including their children continue to face agony.

The report by Chairman Donald W. Reigle, Jr. and Ranking Member Alfonse M. D'amato on "U.S. Chemical and Biological warfare-related dual use exports to Iraq and their possible impact on the health consequences of the Persian Gulf War", submitted to the Senate has compiled massive evidence on the impact of biological and chemical weapons on the armed forces of the United States during the Gulf War, which runs into a large number of pages. This evidence conclusively proves how the American armed forces engaged in the Gulf War are still undergoing pain and agony. Such as they are suffering from recurring headaches, fatigue, joint and muscle pains, memory loss, recurring rashes, lumps under the skin, depression, irritability, night sweats, insomnia, urinary urgency, diarrhea, gastrointestinal problems, dizziness, blurry vision, photo-sensitivity, shortness of breath, coughing, bleeding gums, swollen lymph nodes, seizures, shaking, vomiting, fevers, chest pains, sinus infections and sinus growths. He is 32-year old.[8]

This horrifying story does not end here. The close relatives of these personnel including their wifes and children continue to suffer almost after one decade when they were exposed to the biological and chemical weapons in the Gulf War. The striking features of this report are as follows:

* Iraq intended to use weapons of mass destruction against coalition forces and had the means to deliver these weapons.
* Events did not occur until the air war began.
* There are multiple witnesses to what appear to be best explained as chemical or mixed agent attacks. Symptoms appeared simultaneously with alarms going off, etc.
* Smells, tastes, burning, stinging, numbness are all consistent with chemical or mixed agent attacks.
* Removal and replacement of MOPP gear is consistent with SOP for contaminated equipment.
* Sonic booms are not explosions associated with fireballs and it is unlikely that a commander would order troops not to discuss sonic booms.
* Rates of illnesses are reportedly high in these units.
* Servicemen and women have not received credible explanations of the events from commanding officers.
* The Department of Defence has consistently denied that there is evidence to exposure to chemical and biological warfare agents by US forces, altering its position on specific aspects of this issue only when challenged with evidence that is difficult to dispute.
* The fact that the Sonic Boom explanation was utilized in units subordinate to different services to describe suspicious events and was followed by orders not to discuss the event, suggests that this explanation originated at least at the theatre level. Visual observations reported by field forces suggest this explanation was unrelated to the actual nature of these events.[9]

The question arises why the devastating impact of the chemical and biological weapons on the health of the US armed personnel, later on their relatives and children were either minimized are concealed from the peace-loving American people. This is indeed an intriguing question and no answer can be given to it.

One obvious reason seems to be that use of chemical and biological weapons on the people of Vietnam had created a widespread indignation among the American people. Even today veterans of Vietnam war and their relatives are suffering from a sense of guilt, if one goes by the published materials. This implies the disclosure of the impact of chemical and biological weapons on a section of the American people would have led to serious political repercussion within the country.

Secondly, it would have unmasked the double talk about destruction of chemical and biological weapons by the ruling elite of the United States.

Nevertheless, one thing is certain that Pentagon's attempt to play down the real course of the Gulf War syndrome illness had a political motivation. The disclosure of this sordid aspect of the Gulf War would have established how the Biological Weapon Convention and the Nuremberg Code on Medical Experimentation were violated. The exposure of these facts would have created a mass revulsion within the United States in the Western World and in the entire world. However, one cannot suppress the truth for long and permanently. In the final analysis it is the truth which will prevail.

REFERENCES

1. Dr. Rajiv Nayan, Strategic Analysis: March, 1998.
2. United States, Department of the Army, Field Manual 100-5, Operations (Washington D.C. US Army, August 1982) 7-13 Joachim Krause and Charles K Mallory, Chemical Weapons in Soviet Military Doctrine Military and Historical Experience 1915-91, 2-4.
3. A Congressional Record, 103 Congress, Second Session, Vol. 140, No. 30 Senator Shelby's Conclusions on the Persian Gulf Syndrome (March 17, 1994) S 3098-S 3106.
4. Services Operational Requirement for an Advanced Chemical Agent Detector Alarm 85.
5. According to the manufacturer of the M8A1 Automatic Chemical Detection Alarm the G-Agent sensitivity requirement is that the alarm must sound within 2 minutes when exposed to 0.1 milligram per cubic meter. The M8A1 alarm does not detect chemical bluster agents.

6. Excerpts from a report of Chairman Donald W. Riegle, Jr. and Ranking Member Alfonse M.D'amato of the Committee on Banking, Housing and Urban Affairs with Respect to Export Administration, United States Senate, May 25, 1994.
7. Testimony before the Senate Committee on Armed Services, Subcommittee on Force Structure and Personnel (June 30, 1993).
8. A report of Chairman Donald W. Reigle and Ranking Member Alfonse M.D'amato of the Committee on Banking, Housing and Urban Affairs with Respect to Export Administration, United States Senate, May 26, 1994, p. 84.
9. *Ibid.*, pp. 84-85.

6

Half-truth

In the recent years, a new phrase 'the globalisation and interdependence of the world' has entered the currency of journalistic jargon and academic discourse. The political elite too has begun to use this phrase very often. However, the real significance of this formulation has not yet acquired a precise definition. It will not be incorrect to say that the political elite in the world has yet to grasp the significance of the phrase of interdependence of the world. Perhaps, never before in the present century the content of this concept stood out in a bold relief as it did during the last years of this century. The recent developments such as the Gulf War, Arab-Israel conflict, tension between India and Pakistan graphically illustrate that... irrespective of their caste, creed, religion, political affiliations and the boundaries of their states, our planet has already been transformed into a big spaceship, in which each state and each region have become its integral part. If one accepts the real significance of this transformation of our planet and thereof the content of 'interdependents', the inevitable conclusion will be that if one compartment of this spaceship blows up, the entire ship will crumble down into pieces. It is in this context that one should look at the serious consequences flowing from the use and stockpile of all weapons of mass destruction.

A Close Study of the Gulf War

A close study of the various facets of the Gulf War and use of chemical and biological weapons reinforce this conclusion. Though we shall discuss how Iraq came to possess these weapons of mass destruction and what was the motivation behind the game of turning Iraq into a country possessing biological and chemical weapons, later on, this study in no way minimizes the dangerous policy which the Iraqi ruling elite followed on this sensitive question.

It should be frankly admitted that there were serious concerns expressed prior to the Persian Gulf War about the fallout that would be caused by the bombing of Iraqi chemical, biological, and nuclear weapons production facilities, storage depots, and bunkers.

US military doctrine warns that, according to its calculations, the use of a nerve agent against a target area of no more than a dozen hectares (a hectare is about 2.47 acres) can, under certain weather conditions, create a hazard zone downwind of up to 100 kilometers in length. Within this downwind area, friendly military units would have to take protective measures.[1] The amount of agent and materials targeted during the coalition bombings in Iraq exceeded the amounts by multiples and in magnitude. This fact is relevant to understand the fallout of the use of a nerve agent.

The dispersal of the chemical agents and other hazardous substances is controlled by factors such as topography, wind velocity, direction, temperature, precipitation, vertical temperature gradient and atmospheric humidity. These factors will all contribute to the size and type of dispersal pattern which will be observed.[2] US satellite imagery confirms that debris from the coalition bombings was upwardly dispersed, rather than downwardly dispersed as would occur in offensive use, causing chemical agents to be carried by upper atmospheric currents and distributing trace amounts of chemical fallout over down weather positions. Material distributed from the destruction of the ammunition bunkers and storage depots also travelled upward and outward as confirmed in videotaped records of the destruction of these bunkers obtained by experts. These concerns relating to the fallout from the destruction of these materials were expressed by several credible sources. Let us mention some of them:

1. As a result of these concerns prior to the war, several of the US national laboratories were consulted and prepared reports for the US Army, the US Air Force, and the Department of Energy, advising of the hazards which were associated with bombing these facilities.[3]

2. On February 4, 1991, media sources reported that General Raymond Germanos, a spokesperson for the French Ministry of Defence, confirmed that chemical fallout—probably neurotoxins— had been detected in small quantities, a little bit everywhere, from allied air attacks of Iraqi chemical weapons facilities and the depots that stored them.[4]

3. In late July, 1993, the Czech Minister of Defence confirmed that a Czechoslovak Federative Republic military chemical decontamination unit assigned to an area near the Saudi-Iraqi border had detected the chemical nerve agent Sarin in the air during the early stages of the Gulf War. In this unit, 18 of 169 individuals are believed to be suffering from Gulf War illnesses.[5]

The Czech Chemical Defence Unit in the Persian Gulf in its report has underlined that "during the period after the commencement of the war on January 17, 1991, borderline concentrations of poisonous substances were identified in the air by our chemical surveillance ... during the period from January 1, 1991 until February 28, 1991, it specifically states."

During this period borderline life-threatening concentrations of the chemical agents yperite and sarin were identified several times in both areas of the brigades and in King Khalid Military City (in the military encampment where the unit was stationed) probably the result of the Allies' air attacks on the storage facilities of chemical ammunition in the territory of Iraq. This information had been published at the time in the Czechoslovak media.

This aforementioned fact was confirmed by members of the battalion, chemical defence specialists who evaluated and ordered measures for personal protection. But more revealing is another finding of this report. It has underlined that "it has been proven that military use of chemical weapons by Iraq did not occur and any such fact would have already have been subjected to extensive investigation by agencies of world peace organizations. One can consider that the data measured could have had origins from industrial facilities or even storage facilities of chemical ammunition that were hit by allied bombardment. This is supported by a report of the unit's commander, and by the direct participants. All members of the unit were equipped with the most modern means of protection against toxic substances. They were fully comparable with the current world standard. Any kind of exposure by these types of toxic substances would manifest itself immediately or in a very short time and nothing of this kind has been reported. Latent damage, if it can even be considered in this group, would surely have been uncovered during exit examinations."

"On the basis of the above mentioned facts, one can conclude that the event cannot in any way be connected with the use of chemical weapons or their use in battlefield activities, and harm to the Czechoslovak anti-chemical defence unit due to the military use of toxic substances could not have occurred.

These conclusions also are supported by health care specialists. Neither at the time of identification of the toxic substances, no later, was any member of the unit put under medical care as a result of exposure at this event. All members of the unit were subjected to a complex examination in military hospitals after their return from the Persian Gulf–primarily in the Central Military Hospital in Prague. Even there, no serious changes caused by demanding climatic conditions or by exposure to toxic substances were identified.

Many veterans of the Persian Gulf conflict later participated in and still participate in activities of the unit in the Czech Republic Army in Yugoslavia. Even at the time of their departure, no one mentioned any problems.

Despite this, as on 31 August, 1993, military doctors had examined 18 Persian Gulf veterans who suffered certain health problems, and three of them remain under a doctor's supervision. So far, in their cases, nothing has been identified beyond routine problems related to similar long-term stays abroad."

During the early phases of the air war, there was extensive media coverage of the coalition bombing of Iraqi chemical, biological, and nuclear facilities. ABC News reported that on January 27, 1991 near the Saudi-Kuwaiti border, elements of the 82nd Airborne Division went through a chemical alert drill that was more than an exercise. According to ABC News coverage, their sensors actually registered traces of chemicals in the air, the result, it appeared, of allied bombing of chemical plants in Iraq. A US medical corpsman told reporters, when that the Air Force bombers hit all the gas places there in Iraq, there's a lot of contamination in the air. Some may have filtered down and set these things off. They are very, very sensitive."[6]

Impact of Chemical and Biological Weapons

The following facts provide significant evidence that coalition forces were exposed to mixed chemical agents as a result of coalition bombings of Iraqi nuclear, chemical and biological facilities and that the fallout from these bombings may be contributing to the health problems currently being suffered by Gulf War veterans.

* Iraqi nuclear, chemical and biological weapons plants and storage sites were priority targets for US and coalition forces and were repeatedly bombed.
* Chemical alarms began sounding and the servicemen were put on chemical alert simultaneously with the beginning of the air war.
* The nature of diesel, oil, etc. did not alter during the air war, suddenly causing the alarms to sound. These substances were present before the initiation of the air war, and did not set off the chemical alarms. (The automatic alarms have no sensitivity control.)
* These chemical alarms are battlefield instruments. Battlefields are full of fumes, propellants, explosives, and so forth. It is difficult to believe that they would have been procured if they were ineffective in this environment.
* US military personnel, and the Czech and French governments have confirmed that the chemical alarms were sounding as the result of nerve agent detection.
* The combination of prevailing wind directions, the open terrain, the lack of structural impediments, and other factors listed above, indicate that chemical and possibly nuclear and biological agents from allied bombings became airborne and were being blown and carried across coalition forces, emplacements along the Saudi-Iraqi and Saudi-Kuwaiti border.
* Chemical nerve agents, such as Sarin and others, are known to have a cumulative effect, i.e., they have a slow rate of detoxification. Little is known about the long-term effects of continuous low levels of exposure. Many of the veterans claiming to be suffering from Gulf War Syndrome are exhibiting symptoms of neurophysical disorders.[7]

These conclusions speak for themselves. The cold and disturbing facts compiled now about the impact of chemical and biological weapons, even when they are not directly used do not immunise those who try to destroy their stockpile and storages through aerial bombardments. This is how the aerial bombardment of Iraq has led to serious health hazards for the American armed forces.

The anxiety of the Pentagon to conceal these facts from the American people has obvious reasons. This study therefore, serves as a warning to the entire humanity, the American people in particular, that overt and covert race to manufacture weapons of mass destruction must end without any further delay. This is the moral of the Gulf War. It is therefore, not incorrect to say that half truth is more dangerous than lie.

REFERENCES

1. United States, Department of the Army, Field Manual 100-5, Operations (Washington, D.C., U.S. Army, August 1982) 7-13, Joachinm Krause and Charles K. Kallory, Chemical Weapons in Soviet Military Doctrine Military and Historical Experience, 1915-91. (Boulder, Co. Westview Press, 1992) pp. 142-43.
2. *Ibid.*
3. Interviews with representatives of Lawrence Livermore National Laboratory, Livermore, California, Sandia National Laboratory, Albuquerque, New Mexico, and Los Alamos National Laboratory, Los Alamos, New Mexico.
4. Chemical Fallout Detected in Iraq, Xinhua General Overseas News Service, February 4, 1991.
5. Deve Parks, Czechs Nerve Gas Detected During Gulf War. The Times Picayune (July 30, 1993) A6, Stanislay Mundil, Czech News Agency and Mlada Fronta Dnes July 29, 1993.
6. Sam Donaldson, This Week with David Brinkley, ABC News (January 27, 1991).
7. A Report of Chairman Donald W. Reigle, Jr. and Ranking Member Alfonse M.D'amato of the Committee on Banking, Housing and Urban Affairs with Respect to Export Administration, United States Senate May 25, 1994, pp. 132-33.

7

Iraqi Chemical and Biological Warfare Capability: How was it Acquired?

Iraq and Prohibited Weapons

Over the last ten years, Iraq, a signatory to both the Geneva Protocols of 1925 (prohibiting the use of poisoned gas) and the Biological Warfare Convention of 1972 (banning biological weapons), has expanded an enormous amount of research and energy in developing these and other prohibited weapons.

Iraq was believed to have been manufacturing mustard gas at a production facility in Samarra since the early 1980s. It also began an extensive programme to produce nerve agent precursor chemicals, taking advantage of its own natural resources. Phosphate mines/industries are at Akashat, Al Qaim, and Rutbah.[1] The Iraqi Al Fallujah gas warfare complex was believed to be capable of producing up to 1,000 tons per month of Sarin, as well as the nerve agent VX. In addition, with the assistance of foreign firms, Iraq developed the capability to experiment with hydrogen cyanide, cyanogen chloride, and lewisite.[2]

By the start of the Gulf War, Iraqi forces had developed chemical delivery capabilities for rifle grenades, 81 mm mortars, 152 mm, 130 mm, and 122 mm artillery rounds bombs; 90 mm air-to-ground rockets, 216 kilogram FROG and 55 kilogram SCUD warheads; and possibly land mines and cruise missiles.[3]

On July 30, 1991 Ambassador Rolf Ekenus, director of the United Nations Special Commission on Iraq (UNSCOM) charged with overseeing the elimination of Iraq's chemical and nuclear arsenals, told the Security Council that UN inspectors had found chemical warheads armed with nerve gas. Mr. Ekus claimed that some warheads found were already fitted onto the SCUD missiles.[4]

In March 1991, Molly Moore reported from Jubaly, Saudi Arabia that Marine Commanders found no indications of chemical weapons stockpiles on the battlefields of Kuwait. According to a Washington Post report that day (March 7, 1991) US intelligence analysts claimed that these weapons never got distributed down to the battlefield from storage sites north of the Euphrates River.[5]

Several press sources carried reports of encounters with chemical mines the 2nd Marine Division during the initial mine field breaching operation on February 24, 1991. According to the *Chicago Tribune,* which interviewed officers and enlisted Marines involved in the operation confirmed positive readings for a nerve agent and for a mustard gas. A detecting device gave the same positive reading. General Keys, the 2nd division commander, and Colonel Livingston, told reporters they believed it was possible that a chemical mine was hit.[6]

British troops also discovered Iraqi chemical mines on the Gulf battlefield, according to Gannet News Services. A British official (not further identified) said that the incident was reported to Prime Minister John Major's War Cabinet but no details were given.[7]

Press reports indicate Iraqi readiness to use these weapons against coalition forces. The *British Sunday Times* reported on January 27, 1991, that American intelligence detected greatly increased activity at Iraq's main chemical plant at Samarra in the last week of December, and the British Ministry of Defence said that the Allies believe that Iraq may have as many as 100,000 artillery shells filled with chemicals and several tons (of bulk agent) stored near the front line. According to the Times report, a British Ministry of Defence official said: "The plant was at peak activity and the chemicals were distributed to the troops in Kuwait and elsewhere in the war theatre". The Times reported that an unnamed Pentagon source said that Hussein had given front-line commanders permission to use these weapons at their discretion, and that it was no longer a question of if, but or when.[8]

Iraqi soldiers captured by the British units also informed the allies that before the war started, Iraq distributed substantial supplies of chemical weapons along the front lines to be held for the ground war.[9]

According to *Newsweek*, US intelligence sources had reported that Saddam Hussein had ordered his commanders to fire chemical weapons as soon as the allies launched a ground offensive.[10] A British signals officer was reported to have said that we were tuned into the Iraqi command radio net.

In April 1993, weapons inspectors from the United Nations confirmed that in Muthanna, 65 miles north-west of Baghdad, Iraq manufactured a form of mustard gas as well as Sarin and Tabun, both nerve agents. This vast desert complex was the nucleus of Iraq's chemical weapons programme. During the allied bombing in the early days of the Gulf War, Muthanna was a priority target. It was repeatedly attacked and production sites were destroyed. As United Nations inspectors attempted to destroy Iraq's chemical weapons arsenal, they discovered bombs, missiles, and chemical weapons of mass destruction spread out across this immense complex. Twenty-eight of these warheads have been drained and destroyed by the UN inspectors.

In addition to Muthanna, chemical agents were destroyed at two airbases: one located 40 miles west of Baghdad and the other located near an Nassiriyah, where a number of 122 mm rockets loaded with Sarin were blown into pieces. According to UNSCOM sources, many of these weapons were hastily deployed prior to the air war and later returned for destruction. The UN has destroyed hundreds of tons of bulk chemical agents and tens of thousands of chemical munitions. In addition, hundreds of thousands of litres of key chemical precursors which have been identified and destroyed include 14,600 litres of DF: 121,000 litres of D4 and 153,983 liters of thiodiglycol.

It was also believed that in 1984 Iraq may have used mixed agent weapons with biological tricotnecenes and mycotoxins against Majnoon Island during the Iran-Iraq war.[11]

According to the official military announcements made in the last half of January 1991 and based on the quantity of chemical agents observed by UN inspectors after the war, the scope of coalition bombing against these facilities involved hundreds—if not thousands—of tons of bulk chemical nerve agents, mustard gas, as well as tens of thousands of pieces of chemical munitions. This quantity of chemical warfare agents vastly exceeds the amounts that might be expected to be deployed by a military force in a single chemical attack.

Nerve agents kill by disrupting the metabolic processes causing a build-up of a chemical messenger (acetylocholine) by inhibiting the production of acetylcholine-esterase, a key regulat or of neurotransmission. Lethal exposure to chemical nerve agents is generally characterized by drooling, sweating, crampting, vomiting, confusion, irregular heartbeat, convulsions, loss of consciousness and coma.[12]

Iraq's Biological Warfare Programme

According to the UN, the Iraqi biological warfare programme was initiated in mid-1986 at Salman Pak. UNSCOM inspectors discovered evidence of research into certain biological agents including botulinum toxin and Anthra x as well as organisms responsible for gas gangerene, tetanus and brucellosis, components of a biological weapons programme which was not defensive in nature.

This brings us to the question how Iraq acquired the capability of manufacturing chemical and biological weapons? One can draw conclusion on the basis of available data and information. Records available from the supplies of strategic materials by the United States are revealing. The supplies for the period from 1985 until late eighties show that during this time, pathogenic (meaning disease producing) toxigenic (meaning poisonous) and other biological research materials were exported to Iraq pursuant to application and licensing by the US Department of Commerce. Records prior to 1985 are unavailable, according to the supplier.

These exported biological materials were not diluted or weakened. They were capable of reproducing. Thus by the time of the invasion of Kuwait, Iraq had developed biological weapons. Its advanced and aggressive biological warfare program was the most advanced in the Arab World. The program probably began late in the 1970s and concentrated on the development of two agents, botulinum toxin and Anthrax bacteria. Large scale production of these agents began in 1989 at four facilities near Baghdad. Delivery means for biological agents ranged from simple aerial bombs and artillery rockets to surface-to-surface missiles.[13]

We will come to this question in more details on the basis of media reports. Included in the approved sales are the following biological materials (which have been considered by various nations for use in war) with their associated disease symptoms.[14]

1. Let us at this stage examine what type of material was exported to Iraq before Iran-Iraq war.

1. Bacillus anthracis. Anthrax is a disease-producing bacteria. This material was allegedly used in the Persian Gulf War.

Anthrax is an often-fatal infectious disease caused by ingestion of spores. It begins abruptly with high fever, difficulty in breathing, and chest pain. The disease eventually results in septicemia (blood poisoning), and the mortality is high. Once septicemia is advanced, antibiotic therapy may prove useless, probably because the exotoxins remain despite the death of the bacteria.

2. Clostridium botulinum . A bacterial source of botulinum toxin, which causes vomiting, constipation, thirst, general weakness, headache, fever, dizziness, double vision, dilation of the pupils and paralysis of the musles involving swallowing. It is often fatal.

3. Histoplasma capsulatum. Causes a disease superficially resembling tuberculosis that may cause pneumonia, enlargement of the liver and spleen, anemia, an influenza-like illness and an acute inflammatory skin disease marked by tender red nodules, usually on the shins. Reactivated infection usually involves the lungs, the brian, spinal membrances, heart, peritoneum and the adrenals.

4. Brucella melitensis. A bacteria which can cause chronic fatigue, loss of appetite, profuce sweating when at rest, pain in joints and muscles, insomnia, nausea and damage to major organs.

5. Clostridium perfringens. A highly toxic bacteria which causes gas gangrene. The bacteria produce toxins that move along muscle bundles in the body killing cells and producing necrotic tissue that is then favourable for further growth of the bacteria itself. Eventually, these toxins and bacteria enter the bloodstream and cause a systemic illness.

In addition several shipments of Escherichia coli and genetic materials as well as human and bacterial DNA were shipped directly to the Iraq Atomic Energy Commission.

These exports of strategic materials to Iraq for manufacturing chemical and biological weapons clearly confirms as to who enabled Baghdad to develop these weapons of mass destruction. But this alone doesn't tell the whole story, for almost five years from mid-1985 different types of strategic materials, were exported from the United States to Iraq, if one fully examines the various sources. At least 50 consignments of such materials were sent to Iraq. These facts have been partially reported in the American media (Emphasis added).

As late as on 10 February 1994 the American media reported that during the 1980s ''the US government approved shipment of biological agents to Iraq that could be the cause of the debilitating illness plaguing Persian Gulf War veterans.

''The viruses and bacteria, commonly used to develop biological weapons, were shipped to Iraqi government agencies by American Type Culture Collection, a non-profit group in Rockville that collects and distributes biological specimens worldwide.

"Virtually all the shipments were approved by the Reagan administration's Commerce Department between 1985 and 1989 despite longstanding suspicions that Iraq has been involved in biological warfare.

"While not faulting the Rockville suppliers, the government's action in approving the transactions violates every standard of logic and common sense.

But there is something more to it.

"Richard Roblin, associate science director for American Type Culture Collection, said his group had sent two types of dangerous specimens to Iraq after receiving a request from Iraqi government representatives. One was *Bacillus anthracis,* the organism that causes anthrax, an often fatal ailment. The other was *Clostridium botulinum,* the organism producing botulinum toxin that can cause vomiting, constipation, weakness and headaches. Reigle also names several other biological agents that had been exported.

"We don't make decisions about which cultures are shipped there said Roblin, whose firm is one of the nations largest biological specimen banks and acts as a clearinghouse for scientists. We rely on the Department of Commerce. It's their job".

Iraqi requests for specimens were routinely approved by Commerce's Bureau of Export Administration. During the Reagan administration, the department routinely approved many foreign requests for sensitive materials, even from potential adversaries.[15]

No further evidence and documentation are needed to prove that it was primarily the American Administration which provided strategic material to Iraq to manufacture chemical and biological weapons of mass destruction. But there were other nations too who made their contribution in transforming Iraq into a country possessing stockpiles of biological and chemical weapons. Let us examine this aspect.

"The Iraqi purchases between 1985 and 1989 followed a pattern common to the country's other acquisitions of sensitive Western technology. An initial order was placed for a plant pathogen that causes smut diseases. Dipping a toe into more risky water a few months later, Iraq's ministry of higher education ordered two specimens of a Class III fungus well outside the typical range of biowarfare agents.

"The country's success emboldened it to take a plunge into the most sensitive end of the bacterial pool with a 1986 order for 24 pathogens, including 13 more bacteria designated Class III. That shipment, which like the others received rapid approval from the US Commerce Department included the specific strains of anthrax, Clostridium botulinum, and Clostridium perfringens that Iraq later selected for mass production as germ weapons. All were sent to the University of Baghdad, but secretly paid for by the military, according to Iraqi records turned over to the United Nations.

"The anthrax strain had a British military pedigree which Iraq was doubtless aware of—that illustrates how casually such germs are passed around among scientists and how easily they can be shifted from, innocent to nefarious use. The head of Britain's germ welfare programme had obtained it from an academic researcher and sent it to one of his aides, who eventually sold it to the Rockville repository, where it was swiftly advertised for sale.

"At least three of the other strains Iraq purchased were plainly listed in the repository's catalogue as coming from the US military's biological warfare programme, a factor that doubtless made them of great interest to the ambitious managers of the Iraqi program. Baghdad also successfully ordered other deadly pathogen from the Pasteur Institute in Paris and tried—but failed—to order germs directly from Britain's Military Research Centre at Porton Down in 1988.

"Given the right temperature and enough growth media even the few drops of bacteria in these samples can grow into the basis of a national arsenal of disease. So Iraq placed orders in 1987 and 1988 with the Oxoid firm in Bedford, England, for example, that it made enough botulinum toxin in 1989, 1990 and 1991 in theory to wipe out the Earth's population several times over, and UN officials said that Iraq's actual production may have been two to three times that amount. Iraq has also acknowledged making enough deadly anthrax and Clostridium perfringens to kill or maim billions of people, packing much of these germs into bombs that were secretly distributed to military commanders and deployed with military planes during the Gulf War, and then successfully hidden from inspection teams after the war.

"Biological weapons have long been known as the poor man's atomic bomb because they are cheaper and easier to make than nuclear arms and virtually as deadly.

Once this was accomplished, the programme's emphasis shifted from research towards large-scale production, under the direction of two British-trained scientists; Gen. Amer Sadi, who obtained a masters in chemistry from Oxford University and Rihab Taha who had a doctorate in microbiology from East Anglia University.

"Iraq purchased strains of anthrax and botulinum toxin from a biological supply outfit in Rockville, for example several fermenters used to grow the germs were supplied by well-known firm in Italy and Switzerland, which never suspected Iraq's real aim. A third firm in Germany evidently knew what the fermenter it supplied was to be used for UN officials said."[16]

The question arises why Iraq was overtly and covertly encouraged to manufacture and develop chemical and biological weapons. This is a pertinent question and needs to be investigated. One obvious reason for this was that this strategy was evolved to drive a wedge between Iran and Iraq. Both these countries are rich in oil wealth. They have built over the years an industrial base. They have also a fairly developed agricultural sector. Above all they have a well trained army. As a matter of fact in the Middle East these two countries hold a key position. The political elite of both these countries have their own political ambition, the most important being to seize the leadership of the Islamic world.

That being the position both geopolitical and geoeconomic interest of the United States demanded that these two countries should be weakened militarily, economically and politically. The prolonged Iraq-Iran war created new possibilities to achieve this objective. Therefore, in the mid-80s Iraq was encouraged and helped to possess and develop chemical and biological weapons. But when Iraq and Iran, despite prolonged war were not destabilized, the strategy of US changed. This country became the target and sanctions were imposed on it, which have played havoc with the economy of the country. The people of Iraq are suffering and their children cannot be provided with minimum needs of life including food and medicine.

The irony of the situation is that those who encouraged, promoted and helped Iraq to manufacture weapons of mass destruction are today penalizing it. They have double standards on destruction of chemical and biological weapons. You encourage and help a country to manufacture chemical and biological weapons and then use military threats and economic sanctions to pressure the country to destroy her stockpiles.

To say this doesn't mean that Iraq's path of possessing and developing weapons of mass destruction can be justified in any manner. The international community has asserted itself to make Iraq to destroy these weapons. How far these weapons have been destroyed is anybody's guess. But one cannot ignore the dubious role played by the Western countries, the US and Great Britain in particular. The developing countries should draw appropriate lesson from the tragedy of Iraq and learn to follow an independent policy.

REFERENCES

1. Task Force on Terrorism and Unconventional Warfare. Chemical weapons in the 'Third World, 2, Iraq's expanding chemical arsenal, House republican research committee US House of Representatives (May 29, 1990) 9-10 Anthony H-Crodesman, After the Storm the changing military balance in the Middle East (Boulder and San Francisco Westview Press, 1993) 497-98.
2. Peter Dunn, the chemical war journey to Iran. NBC Defence and Technology International, pp. 28-37, W Seth Carus. The Geme Unleashed Iraq's Chemical and Biological Weapons production, (Washington: Washington Institute policy papers No. 14) 22-23. Foreign Report (March 31,1988) 12 Jane's Defence Weekly (January 9, 1988) 3. Janese's Defence Weekly February 27, 1988) 336, Anthony H Cordesman After the storm the Changing military balance in the Middle east (Boulder and San Francisco Westview Press 1993) 498-546.
3. Michael Eisenstadt, The sword the Arabs; Iraq's Strategic Weapons (Washington: Washington Institute Policy Papers No. 21 September 1990) 7: Seth Carus, Chemical Weapons in the Middle East, Policy Focus, No.9 Washington Institute for Near East policy (December 1988) 4: Iraq's scare tactic, Newsweek (August 2, 1982) In mideast, warfare of a new nature chemical arms, ballistic missiles mark New nature of mideast warfare, *The Washington Post* (April 5, 1988) A1 Dick Palowski, Changes in threat air combat doctrine and force structure, 24th Edition (fort worth: general dynamics DWIC-91, February

1992), 11-325, 11-334, Janeks Soviet intelligence Review (June 1989) 256; Foreign Report (March 31, 1988), 1: *New York Times* (November 12, 1991; as cited in balance in the Middle East (Boulder and San Francisco Westview Press, 1993 a) 499, 547.

4. Frank J-Prial, UN team finds chemical arms four times greater than Iraq claims, *New York Times* (July, 31, 1991) A1.
5. Rick Atkinson. No chemical arms found on battlefield : US says Iraqi logistics failed, *The Washington Post* (March 7, 1991) A1.
6. Colin Nickerson, *War Diary from Chaos and Fear*—A Victory (The Boston Globe, March 3, 1991).1
7. *USA Today* (March 1, 1991) 3A, War Log Gannett Company Inc. International Edition. (March 1, 1991), A 3.
8. James Adams and Andrew Alderson, Strategic View from the Saddam Bunker. The *Times Newspapers, Ltd.* February 2, 1991, British Paper says Saddam Husscin Approved the Use of Chemical Weapons. *Reuters*, (February 2, 1991) A.M. Cycle.
9. Jesse Birnbaum, The Prisoners, *Time Magazine* (March 4, 1991).
10. Tom Masland and Douglas Walker, Are we ready for chemical war? *Newsweek* (March : 1991)
11. H. Kadivar and SC 1, Adams Treatment of Chemical and Biological Warfare Injuries, Insights Derived from the 1984. Attack on Majnoon Island. Military Medicine, (April, 1991) 171-7.
12. William Booth, Gas masks, Antidote cause three deaths and illness in Israel, *The Washington Post* (January 19, 1991) A20,
13. Department of Defence Conduct of the Persian Gulf War, Final report to Congress (April 1992).
14. Terry J. Gander ed., Jane's NBC protection equipment 1991-92, (Surrey, UK Jane's information group, 1992) 3–12 Dorland's *Pocket Medical Dictionary*, 24th edition (Philadelphia W.B. Saunders Col, 1989) James A.F. Compton, Military chemical and biological agents—Chemical and toxicological properties (Caldwell, NJ the Telford Press, September 1987).
15. *The Washington Post*, February, 10, 1994.
16. *The Washington Post*, November 21, 1997.

8

Washington's ResistAnce to Elimination of Chemical and Biological Weapons

Threat of mass destruction by chemical and biological weapons still looms large and till recently the Administration of the US has been resisting the moves for complete elimination and destruction of chemical and biological weapons. As has been mentioned earlier in this study, the American use of chemical weapons in Indochinese region in the 60s and early 70s unleashed a mass indignation among the American people.

"One might ponder the official reasons Washington gives for our fighting in Vietnam, and think: These reasons are so bad that we must have fallen into the hands of fools. But one might also think: These reasons are so bad that there must be other reasons.

The second thought is better.

Other reasons exist. There seem, in fact, to be several grades and varieties of *raisons de guerrilla* that overlie one another like so many geologic strata the softer reasons lying at the surface, and the harder, the stronger ones, below it. So we must do some strip-mining peel away the top propaganda layer to expose the firmer underlying layers of ideology that give the propaganda as its ground-base and purpose."[1]

This is how the peace-loving American intellectuals described the situation and the policies of the American Administration 27 years ago. This assessment holds good even today, if one goes through the international materials on the various initiatives taken for the complete elimination of all weapons of mass destruction.

Before we do that, let us do some 'strip mining' to unmask the ground base of the American policy on this crucial subject, which has a direct bearing on the entire humanity. It is pertinent to recapitulate how an honest American looks at this problem.

"Every master of a global empire since has found occasion to dust off what we now call the domino theory. The theory's implicit description of the way in which the demand for change emerges and is shaped by international events is primitive, paranoid, and mechanistic. But its most fundamental assumption still seems sound: Nationalism is a threat to imperialism...For the moment, we need only note that its popular version begs or circles all the really important social questions on which Westerners generally and Americans in particular are in such need of enlightenment. In stability more important than social justice? Can change be managed within the status quo? Can Western acquisition of global economic hegemony coexist with the just aspirations of small states? Can the progress of that acquisition be reversed without violence? The domino theory has nothing to say about the very conditions and problems that give it the lame life it has. It pretends that there are no questions at all to ask about our extremely advanced international positions; with infuriating arrogance it depicts all the other dominoes as possessions of the Free World, which, being possessed by us, are ours to lose; and implicitly denying that men revolt for human cause, it implicitly outlaws rebellion as a criminal if not diabolic act. Generally, it evokes the images of a very legendary threat, wants us to believe that there is a Gate and that the Enemy is at it—or about to be. There is a struggle in the world. That struggle very much does involve America. And that struggle needs to be understood. ...A good people have been given no chance to wonder who their enemy is and why their enemy fights; have been given no time to think through the astounding implications of a foreign policy which has crept upon them without being explained or debated, a foreign policy which Gary Porter, borrowing from Walter Lippmann and George Ball, has aptly termed "globalism— the ideology of total world involvement."[2]

This 'strip mining' by an American has been quoted not to raise anti-Americanism. The purpose of this is to unmask the hegemonistic ambitions of the American Administration and that too after the Cold War has ended and the Soviet Union has disintegrated. We have to analyse the real truth to see why the American Administration has been following a dubious policy on the biological and chemical weapons of mass destruction. The basic assumption of the American policy makers is that they are the defenders of democracy and human rights and, therefore, the history has assigned them the role of providing leadership to the world. It is this new theory of providing 'leadership' to the world which is being used to mislead the people, the American people in particular, about various facets of Washington's policy, including its determination to monopolise the weapons of mass destruction. This is the basic ground, the hard ground, on which the various moves and counter moves need to be analysed.

Let us examine in this context the various initiatives to ban the use, export and development of chemical and biological weapons since the Vietnam War and the Gulf War.

As a consequence of the developments mentioned earlier renewed attention to the problem of chemical warfare, the Eighteen-Nation Committee on Disarmament (ENDC) placed the issue on its provisional agenda in 1968 under the heading "Non-Nuclear Measures". This came after the conclusion of the Nuclear Non-Proliferation Treaty in the same year. In 1969, for the first time, the "Question of Chemical and Biological Weapons" was put on the agenda of the UN General Assembly.

Following a request by the UN General Assembly in 1968, the UN Secretary-General appointed a group of experts to study the effects of chemical and biological weapons. The report of the group was published in 1969 and was discussed in the ENDC. It described the basic characteristics of chemical and biological weapons, their effects on military and civilian persons, environmental factors influencing the effect of Chemical and Biological Weapons (CBW), possible long-term effects on human health and ecology, and economic and security implications of the development, acquisition and use of chemical or biological weapons. The conclusions of the report were as follows:

"Certain CBW are potentially unconfined in their effects in space and time. CBW could have grave and irreversible effects on the balance of nature. These effects would apply both to the attacker and the attacked. No defence system is completely effective. CBW are no cheap substitute for other weapons, and their elimination would not detract from a country's security. Attached to the report was a recommendation by the UN Secretary-General. It urged States which had no done so to adhere to or ratify the Geneva Protocol. It stated that all chemical and biological weapons (including tear gas and herbicides) should be covered by the Protocol, and that a comprehensive ban should be negotiated."

Another important document, published in 1970 as a contribution to efforts for chemical disarmament, was the WHO report on health aspects of the use of chemical and biological weapons.[3] Its emphasis was on public health and the approach was therefore different compared to the report by the UN Secretary-General. It was of a more technical nature and was directed primarily at public health and medical authorities. Still, the conclusions were essentially the same as those of the UN report.

Strengthening the Geneva Protocol

In addition to seeking a total ban on chemical and biological weapons, many countries thought that it was necessary to strengthen the Geneva Protocol of 1925. International pressure to ensure universal adherence to the Protocol was growing and a number of General Assembly resolutions were passed. They invited all States which had not done so, to adhere to ratify, or accede to the Protocol. Similar calls were made by NGOs for example the ICRC.

These calls were particularly addressed to the United States—the only great power not yet a party to the agreement. China, France (dispository of the Protocol), the Soviet Union and the United Kingdom had ratified or acceded to the Protocol by 1930.

The absence of the United States was thought to be of great significance because it was known to have a large CBW programme and had used chemicals on a large scale in the Indo-China War. The United States argued that it respected the principles of the Protocol but resisted formal commitments. However, international as well as national public opinion caused a change in this position.

On 25 November 1969, the US President issued a statement which contained the following elements:[4]

(a) It reaffirmed the renunciation by the United States of the first-use of lethal chemical weapons.

(b) It extended this renunciation of first-use to incapacitating chemicals.

(c) It announced that the Geneva Protocol would be submitted to the US Senate for advice and consent to ratification.

Later on, it became clear that tear gas and herbicides were not covered by this announcement. The statement also contained a declaration on the unilateral biological disarmament by the United States.

(a) It renounced the use of lethal biological weapons and all other methods of biological warfare.

(b) It confined biological research to defensive purpose such as immunization and safety measures.

(c) It announced that the United States would dispose of existing biological weapons stockpiles.[5]

On 14 February 1970, the United States additionally renounced the offensive preparation and use of toxins for war purposes. Toxins are substances produced by living organisms, including plants, animals and bacteria. Unlike, the organisms which produce them, toxins are not capable of reproduction. The United States stated that military programmes in this field would be confined to research for defensive purposes, and that all US stockpiles of toxin weapons which were not required for defensive research would be destroyed.[6]

The ratification of the Geneva Protocol by the United States was, however, not achieved until 1975 because the Senate Foreign Relations Committee demanded ratification without reservations. The administration, on the other hand sought to exclude riot control agents and herbicides.

The main argument for not covering these substances under the Protocol was that they were widely used for domestic purposes. The use of chemicals which existed in large quantities in many countries could not be prohibited effectively. Another reason sometimes given was that the use of irritants could lead to fewer casualties, including on the side of the enemy.

Arguments used by advocates of the prohibition of these substances for war purposes were that: there is no clear demarcation between irritant agents and other chemicals. The military use of tear gas is different from its civil use. Irritants are often employed to increase the effectiveness of other weapons.[7] The use of these chemicals may also lead to an escalation of chemical warfare in an armed conflict. Herbicides may inflict damage on people and cause a disruption of the ecological equilibrium (including long-term consequences). Additionally, the negotiating history was said to support the comprehensive scope of the Protocol.

In 1969, a UN General Assembly resolution,[8] already referred to, put forward a formal definition of chemical weapons. It included irritant agents and herbicides. It was adopted with 80 votes in favour, three against (Australia, Portugal and the United States) and 36 abstentions (including most Western States).

In 1974, the United States changed its position and US President Ford issued an executive order, still in force, which stated that herbicides could be used by US forces in armed conflict to clear vegetation around US bases. Tear gas may be used to prevent casualties (rescue operation, for example) and for riot-control in prisoners of war camps. The same points were made by the US Senate in 1975 in the context of the debate on the ratification of the Geneva Protocol.

The ratification by the United States, although with a reservation, and the resolution of the dispute over irritants and herbicides strengthened the authority of the Geneva Protocol. However, the problem of formal reservations to the Protocol and especially the question of how to deal with allegations of infection of the agreement remained. Efforts to resolve the latter started in the early 1980s *intensifying efforts to reach a total ban on chemical and biological weapons, and the conclusion of the BWC in 1972.*

Since the end of the 1960s the question of a comprehensive ban on chemical and biological weapons received increasing attention in the ENDC and its successor, the CCD (Conference of the Committee on Disarmament). One of the principal issues was the possible separation of chemical and biological weapons with a view to the development of a legal instrument for their prohibition. A number of Western countries, the UK and USA among them, preferred the elaboration of a convention on biological weapons as a first step since an agreement on CW appeared to be more difficult to achieve.

The United States had unilaterally and unconditionally foresworn the use of biological and toxic weapons and had stated that it would destroy its existing stockpiles. It urged other States to conclude a comprehensive ban on these weapons. A number of countries maintained, however, that these measures were no substitute for a comprehensive treaty.

Negotiations on whether to conclude two separate treaties continued until March 1971. At that time the USSR and other Socialist countries changed their position and accepted the BWC as a first step towards the complete prohibition of chemical and biological weapons.[9] The CCD quickly reached consensus on a joint draft treaty banning the development, production, stockpiling and use of biological and toxin weapons.[10] On 16 December 1971, the UN General Assembly commended the draft treaty on biological weapons.[11] The treaty was opened for signature on 10 April 1972 and entered into force on 26th March 1975[12].

A considerable number of States expressed fears that the conclusion of the BWC would not be followed by a CWC. Therefore, strong commitments relating to further negotiations on a CWC were expressed in the text of the BWC.

Before 1968, the international community always clubbed chemical and biological weapons together. Any effort to deal with one variety had to take care of the other too. When negotiations for the elimination of both varieties of weapons began, the biological weapons were militarily almost redundant, while chemical weapons were much in use. The custodian of contemporary peace—the United States of America—had extensively deployed and applied chemical weapons in the killing fields of Vietnam. By 1972, the conclusion of a Biological Weapons Convention (BWC) became a reality but any such thing for chemical weapons would not find consensus in the community of nations. The attempt towards the CWC certainly got independence and autonomy after the successful conclusion of the BWC, since the all problems, issues and negotiations related to chemical weapons were discussed and dealt with separately.

Different aspects and components of the chemical weapon system involved prolonged negotiations before getting clear-cut definitions enshrined in Article II of the conventions. The USA, the UK, Canada and numerous other countries, in the early 1970s, were not in favour of the inclusion of the irritant agents like tear gas and anti-plant agents in the scope of the convention. But in November 1971, Canada changed its stand slightly while articulating its thinking on the first and retaliatory use of chemical weapons. Its reference to chemical weapons covered all agents to be used against persons, animals and plants. Teargas also figured in the list.

American Chemical Weapons Capability

Binary chemical weapons which gave the USA's chemical stockpile an added advantage, also created a problem in the way of the convention.

America always protested the targetting of binary weapons by the socialist and other countries. It was only owing to an agreement reached between the USA and the USSR in 1974 that binary chemical weapons could be included in the list of ban items. The agreement also covered super-toxic lethal chemicals like phosgene, incapacitants and munitions other than the ones used for smoke dissemination. Again, when the German Democratic Republic (GDR) proposed to start the elimination of binary weapons, to ultimately end chemical weapons, the USA reacted sharply and viewed it as an extremely one-sided intention to destroy the American chemical weapons capability and to preserve the Soviet stockpile. Later the declaration of the Soviet stockpile and intention to destroy it also resolved many of its qualms and the USA gave up its reservations. Drawing up of the three lists of chemicals, which have found a place in the Annexure of the convention, has also been an arduous task. Initially, it was aimed at smoothening the task of verification. A Canadian working paper tried to solve the problem of determining the criteria for different categories of chemicals to be covered and the way these were to be listed in different Schedules. This working paper also gave lists of the chemicals, primarily to help the verification function, that were entirely different from the present three lists of chemicals grouped on the basis of toxicity. In 1989, in the working group of the ADH Committee on Chemical Weapons, the technicalities of relevant chemicals were removed from the general test of the proposed convention and transferred to an Annexure on Chemicals. That Annexure started compiling some of the definitions, the Schedule on chemicals, the modalities for revision of the Schedules and the guidelines and toxicity determinations. Suggestions were made that Schedule 2 should comprise two parts: one for key precursors to actual or potential CW agents listed in Schedule 1 and another for chemicals that might risk the would-be convention.

Destruction of Chemical Weapons

Destruction of chemical weapons was also an important area of continuous disagreement among different countries during the process of negotiations. In 1974, Canada gave the idea of phased destruction of chemical weapons. In 1979, the USA and the USSR agreed to destroy or divert the means of chemical warfare for permitted purposes within ten years of any country becoming party to the CWC. It was proposed that the destruction would be started not later than eight years after any country becomes party to the convention. The size of the accumulated stocks was considered to be the main rationale for the longer time gap. The desire to have a phased elimination was also expressed in this meeting. It was argued by the pro-phase destructions that retention of a certain amount of chemical weapons would determine a non-party and at the same time try to provide the answer to the problem of undeclared hidden stocks. The CWC's concern on safety and the environment was echoed in an Italian suggestion for taking extensive environmental and security measures while destroying stocks of chemical weapons. The measures, according to the proposal, were to apply to the methods of destruction and the duration of the operations in question.

The USA proposed to start destruction of the chemical weapon production and filling facilities not later than six months after the date on which the CWC enters into force. It also favoured that a chemical weapon production or filling facility could be temporarily converted for destruction of chemical weapons stockpile should start not less than eight years once the convention enters into force. In 1987, the negotiators favoured elimination of stocks simultaneously by all states possessing chemical weapons. The degree of harmfulness of the agents and the security of the states parties were the two factors which were considered to be kept in mind, while destroying the agents, during the discussion in the negotiations of that year.[13]

This study based on the official document makes it abundantly clear that all initiatives and moves for elimination and destruction of chemical and biological weapons were initially blocked by the US or diluted. This dilution was done to enable the US to stockpile these weapons of mass destruction. However, the position began to change after the Pentagon came to the conclusion that the American nuclear weapon possession would not allow an adverse impact on its strategic superiority. That is why after the removal of the American opposition to the moves and initiatives for complete elimination of Chemical and Biological Weapons, the chemical weapons in particular created the conditions for decisions by the international community for chemical disarmament. The draft of the Chemical Weapons Convention (CWC) on September 3, 1992, in Geneva clearly confirms this conclusion. This CWC was unanimously endorsed by the UN General Assembly on November 1992. It was opened for signature on 13 January, 1993 in Paris. But once again this ratification did not take place, it took almost four long years that the CWC could come into force on April 29, 1997. What is significant to mention here that the US, China and several other countries deposited their instruments of ratification just a few days before the enforcement of the Convention.

The CWC is commended for its some noteworthy features. Akin to the Biological and Toxin Weapons Convention (BTWC) of 1972, the Convention recommends elimination of an entire class of weapons. Under any and all circumstances, the use of chemical weapons banned. Because of its wide-spread prohibition on all use, production, acquisition, retention and transfer, it is hailed as a comprehensive treaty.

A large number of countries have not filed their declarations. By October 1997, only 68 states party to the Convention had deposited their initial declarations and many of these are incomplete. Shockingly, even the US has provided incomplete details, ostensibly because the Congress has not passed the implementing legislation whereby the US industry is asked to furnish information on the production, consumption, import and export of chemicals controlled by the Convention. Other countries cite other reasons. Although this matter has already been discussed in the Executive Council, it needs to be taken more seriously and assertively. Otherwise it will have negative implications for the implementation of the Convention.

The US, along with nine other countries, had not paid its dues to the OPCW by the end of August 1997. The default of the US, which contributes more than 25 per cent of the total, is really a matter of concern. The Director-General of the OPCW stated that the non-payment of tens of billions of dollars by these countries created a serious financial problem.[14]

Nevertheless the final decision on the selection of alternative technology is awaited. The US, with abundant resources, should be urged to take up the issue more seriously. The American development of the suitable destruction technology will, definitely, be used by other countries. With delay the belief that laxity has crept into the destruction scheme may be perceived.[15]

Moreover, the conditionalities imposed by the US Senate while ratifying the Convention are surely of quasi-reservation nature. It can have wider ramification. The governments of several countries, who have become parties to the Convention in haste or without holding a proper internal debate may be put under pressure to follow the American example.

There is yet another American provocation. Before the American Senate ratified the Convention, the American society had debated security implications of the Convention at great length. Opponents of the Convention cautioned that the CWC would adversely affect American security. Reports of different Western agencies had been quoted to substantiate this by pointing towards some holdout states that have chemical weapons or at least, the potential to produce such weapons. Interestingly a section of the American strategic community has continually been raising the issue of these holdout states. This section projects these countries as security threats and puts pressure on the Administration to reconsider its decision of staying in the Convention.[16]

US President Bill Clinton has given an assurance that nuclear option would be applied if chemical option is used against the country. The same stance was repeated quite recently.

It has also accentuated the general perception that the US never surrenders a weapon that can deprive it of strategic superiority. The new US doctrine might put several other countries under domestic pressure to review their stand on the CWC in relation to security. It can be argued by certain countries which are reluctant to develop relatively costly nuclear weapons that chemical weapons involving low cost and technology will give them a decisive edge over conventional weapons. And the logic would be that if the US cannot surrender its strategic superiority, every other country is also free to take care of its security by preserving whatever strength it has. This can lead to a step towards opting out of the Convention.

This would undermine the promise made in the Preamble of the Convention of working towards general disarmament. The CWC was considered to be a step towards general disarmament. Naturally, nuclear disarmament will be the most desirable component of it. Owing to this goal, several countries went along with the Convention. The American nuclear posture is going to send a wrong signal. It will appear that an important country like the US is not respectful of the basic spirit behind the CWC. The ensuing disillusionment may jeopardise the Convention.[17]

Whatever, the arguments put forth by the supporters of this chemical regime, developing countries do not sight any reason behind the perpetuation of this group. Definitely, there is no wisdom in continuing the regime when the parties to the convention have committed themselves against spread of chemical weapons. Already as parties to the Convention they are not going to use or develop chemical weapon. The history of all export control regimes, including the Australia Group reveals that hegemonic, closed, discriminatory and irrational character of these regimes has failed in stemming the flow of prohibited items and technology. Even Western and American writers are admitting this stark reality.[18]

These regimes have only been successful in troubling and putting obstacles before democratic countries, like India, pursuing an open and transparent policy on transfers. Several countries with dubious track records have been getting away unpunished due to the clandestine transfers of the prohibited technology. More interestingly in the entire process, the biggest help has come through politics of the developed countries. The export control regimes have basically been serving foreign policy goals of the countries like the US.[19]

Now let us examine the impact of biological and toxin weapons and how their proliferation has been taking place. This question has become more relevant today than never before because as we have examined in the previous chapter on the basis of the authentic evidence including a report to the American Senate "on US Chemical and Biological Warfare Related Exports of Material to Iraq from the US". The problem is further compounded by the fact that some other countries too indulged in these exports as published in mass media including in *The Washington Post.*

But before we do that let us understand what really is meant by biological weapons, though we have examined this question earlier in this study, while examining the use of biological weapons (BW) during the Vietnam War.

A BW contains living organisms (as well as the means of their delivery) which is intended for use in warfare to cause death or disease and which for its effect depends on the ability of the organisms to multiply in the person, animal or plant attacked, while toxins are poisonous products of organisms, which unlike biological agents are inanimate and incapable of reproducing themselves. Typically, a BW uses micro-organisms or toxins. While bacteria are single-celled organisms that invade the human body, replicate and cause disease and death, viruses do the same, but are much smaller, consist of genetic material and must invade a host cell to multiply. Poisonous substances that can be synthetically produced or derived from living organisms are toxins.

As already mentioned, biological weapons have been used as weapons of war from early times, when centuries ago soldiers threw plague-infested carcasses over the walls of enemy cities to infect the population. Hostile native Indian tribes were given blankets by White settlers, which were infected with smallpox. It was also used for assassinations for which there are documented cases. More recently, claims have been made that biological weapons were used during World War I and II. Though most of the claims have not been proved, it is known that during and since World War II, dozens of diseases, primarily those caused by viruses or bacteria, have been studied as possible biological weapons. Both the Japanese and the Germans were known to have experimented on prisoners of war.[20]

How does BW compare with other Weapons of Mass Destruction (WMD)? The answers provide an insight why the proliferation of BW is today a very real threat to global arms control and why urgent remedial measures are required towards its non-proliferation. When one considers that it is possible to deliver BW via a water supply with research having shown that it is feasible that drinking 100 ml of water from a reservoir of some 5 million liters capacity would cause serious infection or intoxication if as little as half a kilogram of Salmonella, 5 kg of botulinum toxin, or 7 kg of staphylococcal enterotoxin has been introduced, it becomes clear why possessing BW seems such a viable proposition to vested interests who are inimical to world peace and stability.[21]

Since micro-organisms are the basic material for BW, a fundamental concern is how easily this material can be produced. Also weight-for weight, BW agents can be hundreds to thousands of times more potent than chemical agents and can cause a variety of symptoms. A potential proliferator would find that BW provides a much cheaper route to WMD capability considering the Nuclear Weapon (NW) being very expensive and that BW is much more lethal than an equal quantity of CW. Almost all the technologies and materials required to produce BW are dual-use in nature and are widely available for commercial purposes. As an example, pharmaceutical production techniques can be adopted to produce biological agents. BW, like CW programmes, are much easier to conceal from international inspectors.[22]

Although chemical and biological agents have certain similarities — both are capable of airborne dispersal and are primarily effective against living organisms, whether humans, animals or plants—biological agents have several attractions.[23]

The exponents of the theory of deterrence about acquiring nuclear weapons have to understand that nuclear chemical and biological weapons are weapons of mass destruction and they are components of a system of weaponisation. Any attempt to draw a line of demarcation among these three different systems will not only be unrealistic but will have a serious threat for the security of developing and under-developed countries.

It is not an accident that all these three systems of weapons of mass destruction essentially are monopolised by certain developed countries who want to create an international order which would serve their geopolitical and geoeconomic interests. But there is one more aspect about chemical and biological weapons which needs to be highlighted to understand how complex the problem of disarmament has already become by the end of the present century.

Before we go to this aspect, it will be relevant to mention that chemical weapons can be used by terrorists and divisive forces various too. This has become a material factor if one keeps in mind how developing countries are facing serious threats from terrorists and separatist forces which are patronised by other countries, both morally and materially.

It will not be correct to say that biological and toxin weapons, if given to terrorists, particularly State-sponsored terrorists, they can play havoc. There are some specific instances which confirm this conclusion.

In 1995, for instance, the Government of Myanmar allegedly used biological weapons on the Thai-Myanmar border against the Karen-cthnic minority. Again an extremist group in Japan is believed to have used chemical and biological weapons on experimental basis. Cuba has also alleged that US government used a biological weapon against it by aerially spraying biological agents over farmers to destroy crops. In this sense, on a mini scale, Vietnamese syndrome has begun to unfold itself. All these are portents of dangerous developments.

This study has established beyond any doubt that the US has been blocking the implementation of *Chemical Weapons Convention* CWC as has been analysed earlier. What is more disturbing is that the official evidence has not proved that it has been violating the Convention on the prohibition of the development production and stockpiling of biological and toxin weapons and on their destruction, better known as the biological and toxin weapons convention or by its acronymn BWC. This has been done by exporting strategic material to Iraq to manufacture biological and chemical weapons so that these could be used against Iran.

BWC was negotiated from 1969 to 1971 and was open for signature on April 10, 1972 at London, Moscow and Washington, DC. It came into force on March 26, 1975 with 43 member countries ratifying it.

This treaty has 15 articles. It prohibits the development, production, stockpiling are acquiring by the other means or retention of microbial or other biological agents.

The question arises how and why almost 10 years after BWC came into effect, Iraq developed both biological and chemical weapons and allegedly built their stockpiles. From where did Iraq get the strategic material for this? It is not difficult to answer this question because the Report of US Chemical and Biological Warfare Related Dual Use Exports to Iraq submitted to the American Senate on May 25, 1994 has clearly given an answer to this. The report "is derived entirely from unclassified sources" and has been approved for public release. The report in unmistakable terms has given a mass of facts to show how on various occasions strategic materials were exported to Iraq, which enabled it to manufacture biological and chemical weapons. No other evidence is needed to prove that the administration of the US violated the BWC both in letter and spirit. It is for the international community to draw a line of demarcation between myth and reality, and pretention and practice. Perhaps posterity will give a judgement on it, including the peace-loving American people.

REFERENCES

1. Carl Oglesby and Richard : Containment and Change : p. 7.
2. *Ibid.*, p. 14.
3. Geneva 1970 : WHO.
4. ACDA, Documents on Disarmament 1969, Washington, D.C. 1970, pp. 592-93.
5. A/C. 1/PV-1699.
6. Office of the White House Press Secretary, 14 February, 1970, Press Release, ACDA, Documents on Disarmament 1970, Washington, D.C. 1971, pp. 5-6.

7. E.g. to smoke out the enemy and then to attack him in the open.
8. A/2603 A(XXIV).
9. E.g. CCD/PV.505(USSR), CCD/325 (Socialist countries), CCD/327 (Socialist countries), CCD/339 (Hungary, Mongolia, Poland), CCD/353 (Socialist countries).
10. Official Records of the Disarmament Commission, Supp. for 1971, Doc. DC/234, See also CD/337 (Socialist countries) CCD/338 (USA).
11. A/2826 (XXVI) A/8457.
12. At the end of 1988, there were 110 parties to the BWC. Review conferences of the BWC were held in 1980 and 1986. At the second Review Conference, some limited CBMs were agreed to.
13. *Strategic Analysis*: December 1994 pp. 1119-21.
14. *Strategic Analysis*: March 1998 : pp. 1818-19.
15. *Ibid*., p. 1820.
16. *Ibid*., p. 1821.
17. *Ibid*., p. 1823.
18. *Ibid*., p. 1824.
19. *Ibid*., p. 1825.
20. *Ibid*: September 1997: pp. 875-76.
21. *Ibid.* pp. 877-78.
22. *Ibid.*, p. 878.
23. *Ibid.*, p. 879

9

Iraq's Stockpile of Weapons of Mass Destruction: Myth and Reality

Chemical Weapons free Zones

Throughout the 1980s world public opinion veered round destroying and eliminating chemical weapons. A number of meetings were held to discuss chemical weapons free zones. The United Nations Special Sessions on Disarmament II and III addressed the question. A number of countries seemed to be moving towards acquiring chemical weapons to counter the nuclear weapon capability of their perceived opponent. Iraq was one of them.

The second Gulf War of 1990-91 and Iraq's threat of using chemical weapons changed the whole complexion of the debate. The world suddenly came to realize how a technologically underdeveloped nation, with sufficient funds and the connivance of the chemical and armament industries of the developed world, could clandestinely acquire an enormous arsenal. If it were somehow actually possible for Iraq to use the chemical weapons that it had carefully stockpiled, the fate of the war might perhaps have been different. UN inspections conducted after the war uncovered huge quantities with Iraq.[1]

We have analysed earlier how Iraq acquired this capability. Soon after the war ended in May 1991, the question of destruction of these weapons in possession of Iraq came to the forefront. Quite apart from this aspect the disintegration of the Soviet Union from August 1991 gave a new thrust to the demand for destruction of these weapons. However, before we analyse this problem further one more fact should be mentioned.

Iraq's biological and toxin weapons programme has demonstrated that the danger of proliferation of these weapon agents is real. Iraq is subject to the obligations of United Nations Resolution 687. Apart from Iraq, other countries alleged to be potential possessors of BW agents are China, Israel, North Korea, South Africa, Syria; developers—Libya; potential developers—Iran, Taiwan; capable—Belarus; potentially capable—Pakistan or possibly capable—South Korea, of developing such agents.[2]

The question arises why Iraq was singled out for destruction of these weapons notwithstanding the fact that there were other countries too which possessed these weapons or had the capability to acquire these weapons. There are obvious reasons for this.

Conflict between the US and Iraq

Since the Persian Gulf War of 1990, the conflict between the US and Iraq has been becoming sharp. One obvious reason for this was that Washington directed its energies to create conditions to throw out of power the Baath party regime headed by Saddam Hussein. However, when these moves did not materialise the conflict between the US and Iraq deepened. The situation took a serious turn when the Clinton Administration ordered a missile strike against the Iraqi intelligence headquarters in Baghdad. Again in 1994 the American Administration ordered 44 rounds missile strike against southern Iraq when the Iraqi regime supported one Kurdish faction against the other. The conflict between Washington and Baghdad took a serious dimension when the American members of the UN inspection team incharge of destroying Iraq's weapons of mass destruction were refused permission to carry out their assignment.

Threats were held out to Iraq again and again that if it did not destroy weapons of mass destruction, military action would be taken against it. In fact at one stage the Clinton Administration underlined that "time is running out" for diplomacy and the military action had become imminent.[3]

In the midst of fast changing developments in the Gulf region in February 1998, it became difficult to predict whether immediate military action in Iraq was imminent or not. However, one thing was certain that if the American and British ruling circles were determined to verify whether chemical and other weapons of mass destruction were hidden in the huge presidential complex and other such areas. Iraq made it clear that it would defend its sovereignty with all the resources at its disposal. Nonetheless, it reiterated that it would fully cooperate with the international body to verify whether all the weapons of mass destruction had been destroyed or not.

Iraqi Deputy Prime Minister Tariq Aziz had clearly spelt out the stand of his country in various press conferences, which can be summed up as follows :

Firstly, the Iraqis charged that the UNSCOM inspection team as presently constituted was heavily loaded in favour of the United States and Britain.

The 44-member team led by Scott Ritter, a US national included 28 who are classified as arms inspectors. Of the 28 there are 10 US nationals, five Britons, three French, two Austrians and one each from Bosnia-Herzegovina, Brazil, Finland, Germany, India, Ireland, Sweden and Switzerland.

Iraqis felt this team did not reflect the international community and therefore would be biased against Iraq. The composition of the arms inspection team should as far as possible reflect the diversification of the United Nations and should be made up of people from more countries, Chinese Foreign Ministry spokesman Shen Guofang had openly said. This was a significant declaration.

Secondly, Iraq not only had protested on the composition of the team but also had accused Ritter of being a spy for his country. Ritter served with the US-led allied forces against Iraq in the 1991 Gulf War.

Thirdly, Iraq had claimed that the Investigation Team so far had not produced any evidence to show that Iraq had not destroyed weapons of mass destruction including chemical weapons. It had alleged that all the noise which was being created combined with the threats of military action had a clear objective of throwing out of power, the present leadership of Iraq, if possible through political manoeuvres or through military action and that too under the flag of the United Nations.

Fourthly, Iraq's stand was that the problem of complete elimination of weapons of mass destruction should be handled by experts, scientists, technical experts and not by those who have specialized in other areas such as intelligence gathering.

However, the United States and Great Britain were not influenced by these arguments and felt that Iraq should be made to implement the UN resolution.

Iraq felt that it was being made a scapegoat to divert public opinion in the United States because the President was getting involved in various unsavoury controversies.

A last round of diplomacy followed by an ultimatum and then a final blitzkrieg of an incisive air and missile attack were parts of the strategy worked out by President Clinton's top foreign policy makers.

A sustained attack on suspected biological and chemical weapons sites that Baghdad had so far managed to hide from the UN weapons inspectors would form part of the plan. This implied that the Presidential palace would be the main target.

So far Britain had been the only nation offering its unconditional support. The two US battle groups in the Gulf were to be joined by a British battle group to form the most formidable military deployment in the region since the Gulf War.

However, Washington was facing another problem: the global coalition that former President George Bush put together in 1991 was difficult to build in the new world scenario.

Russia, China, France and even some of the Arab countries had made it clear that they were against a military attack on Iraq. Moscow took active steps to defuse the tension between Iraq and the United Nations. Russia and France had opposed the use of force to resolve the crisis, with the hope of putting further pressure on Iraq to allow UN inspection of its weapon sites including Presidential Palace.

This shows that Iraq was on the brink of a precipice. To understand the nature of the explosive situation in the region at that stage, two other factors should be taken into account.

Firstly, West Asia with 15 countries including Egypt, Iran, Iraq, Israel, Jordan, Kuwait, Lebanon, Oman, Palestine, Qatar, Saudi Arabia, Syria, Turkey and UAE, had traditionally been a high-spending region on defence accounting for 5.67 per cent of the global defence expenditure. The high mark levels of the 1980s and early 1990s were a consequence of the wars (Iran-Iraq 1980-88 and Kuwait 1990-91). Iran's military build-up was followed by Iraq starting its own build-up since 1975. Egypt started to rebuild its military and Saudi Arabia from 1979 onward.

One of the major factors for the high level of defence spending in West Asia has been the oil-rich economies, which received a boost after the 1973 oil shock and price rise. In a sense, the petro-dollars are being spent on sophisticated weapons.

This also explains Saudi Arabia constantly spending much of its defense allocations on sophisticated weapons procurement from Western countries.

Iran and Iraq, especially during their long war, were being sold weapons by the industrialised countries. These two countries, for example, had accounted for as much as 40.45 per cent of West Asian defence expenditure for 1987 while for 1996 they accounted for a mere 2.67 per cent. Now Saudi Arabia alone spends about one-third of the total West Asian defence expenditure. Israel the next higher spender accounts for one-fifth of West Asia's total defence spending. Put together Saudi Arabia and Israel account for more than half of West Asian defence expenditure. These two are then followed by Iran and Iraq which were third and fourth in West Asia. This shows that the balance of military spending in this region has undergone major changes.

Saudi Arabia is the highest spender in this region, accounting for 33.75 per cent of the total West Asian defence expenditure in 1996. Israel's security dilemmas may be gauged from the fact that it accounted for 17 per cent of West Asian defence spending as compared to 51.77 per cent by its neighbours.

On the other hand, the view that Iran poses a threat to the Arab states across the Persian Gulf is not sustainable on the basis of facts. In 1996 Iran account for a mere 8.26 per cent of the West Asian defence spending as compared to 51.18 per cent by the Gulf Cooperation Council (GCC), which in addition is supported by a massive US military forces and bases worldwide, the only forces structure to be added to the US military was in the Persian Gulf in the form of the Fifth Fleet.

These statistics speak for themselves. It shows that two states close to the United States are the highest defence spenders. This has brought a change in the geopolitical strategy of the United States, towards Iran and Iraq in particular.

Secondly, the policy of the United States till recently was targeted at Iran, as it was perceived by the Clinton Administration as the chief perpetrator of Muslim fundamentalist terrorism all over the world. However, of late the American perception about Iran's foreign policy has undergone a change for more than one reason. The recent changes in Iran, particularly its orientation to concentrate on building its internal economy has influenced the American policy towards Iran.

There is yet another factor which should be taken into account in assessing the changes in the Persian Gulf Area. Of late, there has been a noticeable shift among the influential members of the foreign policy establishment in the United States. They have begun to argue that the US should adopt a more open minded approach towards Iran. Therefore, Washington appears to have given up the old policy of "dual containment". This policy has its own significance in the sense that the US policy makers no longer put Iran and Iraq on the same footing. There are various factors which have brought about this shift.

One among them is that Iran's relations with Russia and China have begun to grow rapidly. Quite apart from this aspect US cannot afford to ignore the fact that both the European Union and Japan have begun to make investments in Iran. The American policy makers too are interested in expanding their economic relations with Iran in view of its expanding internal market. The new direction in Iran's foreign and economic policy towards Russia, China and India is viewed by US as a move to isolate her in this region. In this connection it is significant to mention that Iran's export in the late 90s to the European Union stood at 17.5 billion US dollars including 1.35 billion US dollars to Italy, 1.1 billion dollars to France, 600 million dollars to Germany and 200 million dollars to the United Kingdom. These exports mainly consist of oil and gas.

In the totality of the situation, therefore, American policy is now directed mainly against Iraq, and perhaps next to it comes Libya. The crux of the matter is that the build-up against Iraq—political, diplomatic and military—conceals more than what it reveals

The Gulf region has once again become a focus of international attention. It is anybody's guess as to what will happen in this region in the coming days. A US team had begun mapping Iraq's presidential compounds with a view to find out if weapons of mass destruction are concealed there or not. Three members of the security council, i.e. Russia, China and France, had in varying degrees opposed the military solution of the problem. The entire Gulf region had expressed deep concern over the likelihood of military operation in Iraq by the US-British alliance. The question arises why US was following a policy of brinkmanship in the Gulf region.

There are no two opinions that all weapons of mass destruction should be destroyed and India has been in the forefront in articulating this demand. Nevertheless, it needs to be underlined that nuclear weapons have no military utility. These weapons are used to pressurise other countries. In fact, the developments of last two decades clearly show that nuclear powers themselves promote some countries to attain nuclear weapon capability.

Firstly, it must be underlined that with steep decline in oil production in the Arab countries, the American policy makers have now directed their attention to oil reserves of Central Asian Republics and to Iran and Iraq which continue to have rich oil reserves. Statistics prove that Central Asian Republics will push themselves ahead of oil rich Gulf countries. At the end of 1993 the reserves-production ratio for these four republics indicates that oil will last for 92 years in Azerbaijan, 124 years in Kazakhstan, 30 years in Turkmenistan and 78 years in Uzbekistan. Turkmenistan with its 2.4 tr.cu.m. gas will compensate for limited oil reserves. This has led to a basic change in America's policy of 'Dual Containment' towards Iran and Iraq.

Secondly, Iran's rocket programme started during 1977-79 under the Iranian-Israeli project "Flower", with range of 480 km. Under the bilateral agreement Israel took an obligation to develop and to test the rocket. Iran provided Israel with oil. In 1978 alone it supplied oil worth 260 million dollars. At that time there was no rocket building industry in Tehran. The rocket system perhaps was transported by a Swiss company. In 1979 the realization of the project came to the test stage when during anti-Shah revolution the new Iran government gave up "Flower" and made public many documents regarding the project. This step led to the tension between the USA and Israel.

The war against Iraq (1980-88) made the Iranian leadership to reconsider its attitude towards rocket weapons. Iran undertook active measures to diversify sources to get rockets, rocket technologies and materials. Since 1980 Syria, North Korea and China have become main suppliers of rocket machinery.

However, this did not mean Tehran gave up purchase of rocket technologies from the West. For instance, in 1985-86 British company "Royal Ordinance" sold solid rocket fuel, explosives to Iran. The most significant violation and attempts of violation of the Missile Technology Control Regime Treaty were made by the states belonging to the regime, including the products of dual usage. Germany's Maqirus Deut for instance supplied to Iran 5000 semi-trailers. It was carried out in collaboration with the Italian "IVECO". The cost of these goods was more than 300 million dollars in 1991. Again German Messershimdt-Belkov-Blomm supplied trucks L-911SB used as launching device for short range missiles to Iran, which have been displayed during military parades in Tehran.

Some American and other Western companies perhaps want to sell to Tehran test equipment designed for the missile project Silkworm, ground satellite station, and cryptographic equipment, if one analyses the strategic material.

However, the US and Israel are accusing Russia of helping Iran to develop its missile programme. According to Western experts, during 1991-93 Russia vigorously supported the USA policy of "double containment" against Iran. It has to be admitted that in 1995 Russia and Iran signed an agreement on supply of equipment and technology for the atomic power station at Bushir. Now Russia is participating in a gas project in Iran which is estimated to be over 2 billion US dollars. This shows Russia has begun to enter those areas of middle east economy where the USA has a deep interest.

Nevertheless, despite the political and ideological differences between US and Iran, the US will increase its military presence in the region.

The USA continued to maintain its economic presence in the region even in the period of highly strained relations and economic sanctions against Iran. The USA continued importing Iranian oil through intermediary sources. The quantity of Iranian oil bought by the US exceeded the import of other countries. It was estimated at 600 thousand barrels.

Supplies of American spare parts of dual usage to Iran costing tens of millions of US dollars through third countries and mediator companies should not be ignored. The explanation of the US administration of not knowing about oil purchases from Iran does not cut ice.

Iranian oil and gas, Caspian oil, Turkmenian gas, uranium, Tajikistan polymetals, as well as transit routes from Europe to the Indian Ocean and from South East Asia and Far East to Europe are the main factors which determine the interest of the US and its allies in this region including towards Iran. Hostility towards Iraq should be seen in this context.

This explains why the Caspian states, including Iran, are considered by the Americans as a zone of their vital interests and special sections on "Caspian problems" have been set up within the US administration. The former US Secretary of State A. Haig has been conducting talks in

Turkmenistan on the construction of pipeline for the supplies of Turkmenian gas via Iran with the participation of American companies.

The US has also undertaken specific steps to strengthen its economic presence in Iran. On 18th April, 1997, Foreign Control Division of the US Ministry of Finance has made an amendment to "Iranian Transactions Regulations". This stipulates that American companies are only to inform the Ministry of Finance about oil operations which quarterly cost one million dollars or above. This implies that American companies have to evolve their deals up to one million dollars without prior sanction. These cold facts speak for themselves.

These facts are being recapitulated so that one can see the propaganda and ideological wrappers of the weapons of mass destruction and the double standards being followed by those who monopolise these weapons, the United States in particular are exposed. This exercise is directed to bring out the firm underlying layer of geoeconomic and geopolitical interests in this specific issue and that too in a period when the next century is going to be the century of the Asia Pacific Region. Let us not make any bones about it. However, it will be naive to believe that hegemonistic ambitions of the United States are not being challenged. Its claim of world leadership is getting eroded. This conclusion is confirmed by recent developments connected with weapons of mass destruction by Iraq.

Anyone who has been closely watching the recent developments connected with liquidation of weapons of mass destruction by Iraq would agree that a brake has been put on the policy of brinkmanship of the United States and Great Britain.

After the Security Council unanimously approved the agreement between UN Secretary General Kofi Annan and Iraq's Deputy Prime Minister Tariq Aziz in the last week of February 1998, certain new developments took place, which underlined the dual policy of US. There were three most important developments which need to be underlined.

Firstly, United Nations Secretary-General had appointed former Indian diplomat Prakash Shah as his adviser on Iraq to coordinate UN policy better in this country. It may be recalled here that after his trip to Baghdad, Mr. Annan had expressed the need for a political advisor to help him coordinate the large UN operations in Iraq and maintain an open communication with the leaders there.

This was a significant step taken by the UN Secretary-General and partly met the demand of Iraq that instead of US dominated inspection team some other mechanism should be evolved.

Secondly, Russia had demanded that a Russian expert should be appointed as a deputy leader of the UNSCOM inspection team with a view to make the composition of this team more balanced. This team was heavily loaded in favour of the United States and Britain.

Thirdly, in meetings with visiting British and French Foreign Ministers. China's Vice Premier and Foreign Minister Qian Qichen emphasised that Beijing was deeply concerned about the accelerating deterioration of the crisis in Iraq and expressed the hope that settlement of the issue should be accomplished through diplomatic channels. China was opposed to both threats to use force and actual use of force to solve this tangle. Almost identical had been the position of France.

However, what was of far reaching significance was that UN Secretary-General Kofi Annan had made a valuable contribution in defusing this situation. He clearly perceived the growing resentment all over the world on the American threat to use force in Iraq.

In fact, it will not be incorrect to say that popular opinion throughout the world including in a section of the American and the British people played a key role in holding back both the American and the British ruling elite from embarking on the path of military operation in Iraq. This in itself underlines that popular opinion in the world has become a key factor in the new international situation. This new feature needs to be emphasised in a period when attempts are being made to build an American dominated unipolar world.

To say this does not mean that one should minimise the American ambitions, notwithstanding the fact that Russia, China and third world countries have once again begun to assert themselves.

After UN Secretary-General Kofi Annan and Iraqi Deputy Prime Minister Tariq Aziz signed an agreement about dismantling Iraqi weapons of mass destruction on February 24, 1998, which was later approved by the UN Security Council, another significant development took place.

UN Secretary-General on March 8, 1998 in an interview said that the US did not have the authority to use force automatically against Iraq even if Baghdad again stalled UN Special Commission (UNSCOM) inspectors from carrying out inspection of suspected weapons. The UN Chief's views were a clear contradiction of US President Bill Clinton's stated position that Washington did not need the permission of UN to strike Iraq for any breach of a deal Baghdad reached with Annan in February.[4]

Nevertheless, the situation continues to be explosive. No one can predict as to what will be the outcome of the current situation in this region. There is a war cloud over the Iraqi sky. The fact is that Washington is facing a dilemma in more than one sense. The Clinton administration has been very frequently threatening to use military force to ensure what it calls Iraqi compliance with UN Security Council Resolutions, if diplomacy fails.

REFERENCES

1. *Asian Strategic Review*, 1993-94, p. 183.
2. *Strategic Analysis*, September 1997, p. 880.
3. *Strategic Analysis*, April 1998, p. 86
4. *National Herald*, Dated 10.3.1998.

10

Chemical-Biological Weapons and Ecology

Universal and complete disarmament including chemical and biological weapons and above all the elimination of nuclear weapons have become the key issue for the survival of the human race. However, various theories and concepts are being advanced to justify their stockpiles particularly by those who virtually have a monopoly on these weapons, the club of five nuclear weapons in particular. India has consistently been demanding in various forums for the complete destruction of these weapons.

The Indian proposals about destruction of chemical and biological weapons are highly important for the solution of other global problems facing the mankind linked with protecting people's health and preserving the environment from the toxic effects of different chemical weapons.

The use of the existing stockpiles of this type of mass destruction weapons for military purposes would lead to a fatal outcome for mankind and it presents a real threat to the environment too. Chemical weapons pose a potential danger to man's health and his surroundings even in peace time: during their testing, manufacturing and stockpiling. This is confirmed by numerous facts.

In January 1983, Ho Chi Minh City, the capital of the Socialist Republic of Vietnam, hosted a highly representative international scientific symposium where scientists and experts from the SRV, the USSR, the USA, Great Britain and many other countries met to discuss a range of questions dealing with the long-term consequences of US aggression in South Vietnam and mapped out the directions of research for eliminating the after effects of US chemical warfare. We have discussed this problem earlier in this study.

US Military in Vietnam

The participants in the symposium came across the first traces of crimes perpetrated by the US military in Vietnam when they stepped out of the plane in Ho Chi Minh Airport. Not far from the runway were the transport airplanes left behind by the US Air Force during its speedy flight from Southeast Asia in 1972. They had been equipped with special devices for chemical warfare and were used to spray South Vietnam with 7,000 tons of irritating toxic agent CS and over 90,000 tons of chemical defoliants.

The chief base of the US Air Force in South Vietnam was stationed in Bien Hoa not far from Ho Chi Minh City. Most of its facilities were preserved up to late eighties. In the years of US aggression Bien Hoa was the site of a field military chemical plant (one of three in this theatre of war) manufacturing Agent Orange and other combat herbicides.

Near Ho Chi Minh City one can see the remains of a US chemical weapons depot which had contained stockpiles of chemical mines, bomb clusters, air-to-surface missiles, diverse grenades, CS gas pot-shots, etc. The participants in the international symposium learned more about the crimes of the US military in Vietnam by studying the exhibits displayed in the unique museum of military history in Ho Chin Minh City.

Yet this material evidence of the crushing defeat of US aggression in Vietnam was not the only thing that brought scientists and experts to this scientific symposium. Ecologists, biologists and physicians working in different fields of medicine were alarmed by the long-standing effects of the large-scale chemical war waged many years ago on the people's health and the environment.

The term scorched earth tactics was coined during the Second World War. It denoted the purposeful devastation of large areas of land by the Nazi invaders, the total eradication of all populated areas along with their housing, industrial and public facilities. The scorched earth tactics were engendered by the criminal policy of the Nazi leaders and its implementation was facilitated by the increased destructive power of weapons, especially towards the end of the Second World War.

In those years these tactics were adopted by the US Armed Forces as well. Suffice it to recall the napalm bombs dropped by the US Air Force on German cities when this was not necessary for war purpose. One cannot forget that single massive air raid on Tokyo when barrels with napalm dropped from US aircrafts destroyed one-third of the city, chiefly its workers districts in a single night. The USA dropped bombs on Hiroshima and Nagasaki immediately alarmed the world: the future of mankind and nature are at stake. We have analysed this tragedy in this study.

All this is nothing new. Nevertheless, before the early 1960s nothing was known of the fact that since 1942 the USA had been testing a radically new type of chemical weapon. It was intended for use not so much against people as against the environment.

In August 1970, condemning the crimes perpetrated by the US Army during its chemical war in Vietnam, US Senator Gaylord Nelson said: "The history of mankind has never known a case in which a country declared war against the environment of another nation; yet the United States embarked on an ecological experiment which no nation else dared undertake".

The USA had long been nurturing plans for waging large scale ecological warfare and had been making intensive preparations to this end. The people of Japan were chosen as its first victim. At the close of the Second World War the USA was stepping up preparations to destroy all of Japan's rice crops so as to leave its people and army without food. Japan capitulated under the decisive attack of the Soviet Army and foiled the plans of US military circles. The USA switched its ecocide weapons to combat national liberation movements. Their main blow was directed against Vietnam.

The massive use of chemical weapons, unprecedented in the history of wars and continued for more than 13 years (including the use of herbicides by the Saigon regime) which had embraced almost a half of South Vietnam and several provinces of Laos and Cambodia, led to unpredictable changes in all the three spheres of the environment: biocenosis (funa and flora), soil and water, and climate.

This was the first time that the participants in the symposium had come across such a host of new scientific and practical problems whose solution was indispensable for eliminating or in some cases at least localising the long-term consequences of the past chemical war. The scientists confined themselves to expressing general hopes for carrying out a comprehensive study of the complex sum total of the newly emerging ecological, medico-biological and other problems. Vietnam's problems drew special attention owing to the fact that many similar problems, if only on a smaller scale, had emerged in the participants' own countries. Among them was the problem of accidents at enterprises that had manufactured products for chemical warfare in Vietnam. The point is that many US soldiers who had taken part in defoliating Vietnamese forests and destroying crops, or in action in contaminated areas had also been affected by Agent Orange and Dioxin. It also turned out that Vietnam's problems were closely linked with those of removing toxic chemical wastes containing Dioxin semi-products formed through synthesis of Agent Orange and other similar toxins.

We have already discussed in this study the impact of chemical and biological weapons on the American soldiers engaged in the Gulf War.

It is common knowledge that the scientific application of herbicides and defoliants benefits mankind by raising crop yields and accelerating the renewal of forests. If used in concentrations hundred times exceeding the tolerable level for combat effect over large areas, these chemicals destroy the biocenosis and in the ultimate end are liable to cause a large scale ecological catastrophe.

Chemical War and Natural Environment

The herbicides and defoliants used in Vietnam had an immediate effect on the country's natural environment: forests and crops were destroyed, wild animals and cattle, birds and poultry, fish, amphibia, insects and even micro-organisms were perished.

The destruction of mountain and plain tropical rain forests cardinally affected the soil, the river regimes and even the climate in several provinces of South Vietnam. Mountain forests had protected the upper soil layers from being washed off by the heavy tropical rains. During the rainy season the undergrowth in these forests had retained much of the rain waters in the soil helping restrain the force of the surface flow. In the dry season these "reserves" made up for the lack of water in nearby rivers and riverlets. Today when the rains come to these forestless areas and torrents gush down unbridled from the mountains, severe droughts set in there during the dry season.

In their final document the participants in the symposium came to the unanimous conclusion that toxic agents sprayed on a large scale, at a high concentration, and in large amount, have changed the composition of some soils, destroyed useful micro-organisms, and in some instances, caused the soil to lose fertility and to deteriorate in other ways. Many areas which had been covered with trees and other woody plants have become savannas of low productivity. They grow only wild grasses or a number of secondary successional plants having little economic value, and support rodents which are disease carriers. Evidence from aerial photography and other sources indicates that some of these savannas are continuing to expand in size. Some species of valuable tropical wood are facing the danger of extermination, as are some precious terrestrial and aquatic animals. Transforming these savannas back to forest or building them into economic zones for agriculture presents difficult problems, the solutions of which are often far beyond the present abilities of the Vietnamese people. Moreover, all the employed means of affecting nature have virtually undermined the country's life-supporting system. The chemical war has greatly affected Vietnam's mangrove forests, the chief natural spawning ground of salt water fish and the home of valuable shell fish used for food. The destruction of these forests has deprived the local population of their traditional food sources forcing many to leave these parts. The restoration of the mangrove forests has just begun and will take much time. The changes in the river flow regime, large-scale soil erosion and sedimentation, as well as toxic residues from herbicides, defoliants, Dioxin and arsenic contained in the water and soil are liable to affect, and to no small extent, the fauna and flora of these forests ecological system.

The US Army had used Agent Orange mixed with Dioxin. In the course of the chemical war not less than 2,000,000 people, chiefly men, were affected by herbicides and Dioxin. To this day the Vietnamese soil contains large residues of herbicides and defoliants, the different technological additives they incorporated including Dioxin, along with the products of their disintegration of the chlorophenol group. These toxic agents are carried by rainwater and ground water to uncontaminated land and water areas, where they join the nutrition cycle and produce damaging effects. Today it is impossible to determine the exact number of people who have come into contact with the Dioxin which has found its way into Vietnam's natural environment since the end of the chemical war.

However, Dioxin produces effect through direct or indirect contact in exactly the same way and to the same extent. Dioxin is a highly toxic organic agent diversely affecting human organs and producing metabolic disturbances. Its teratogenic and carcinogenic properties manifest themselves in the human organism upon contact with the most mini-scale doses of this agent.

The Summary Report of Working Group on Cancer and Clinical Epidemiology came to the general conclusion, that there is general consistency between the pattern of chronic toxicity induced in animals by Dioxin and Dioxin-contaminated chlorophenolic compounds and those observed in exposed human populations. Such toxicity includes: (1) chronic hepatitis, (2) disturbances in immune function, (3) disturbances in lipid and porphyrin metabolism, and (4) neurological abnormalities, sometimes associated with a toxic neurasthenic syndrome.

Dioxin's Toxic Effects

Medical statistics show that Dioxin's toxic effects could be observed many years after ending of the chemical war and there is every danger that they will continue to recur. Thus after the war the number of children with in-born deformities was ten times higher in South Vietnam, where Agent Orange and Dioxin were used, than in North Vietnam, where they were not (4 and 0.4 per cent respectively). Examination of 956 families where the husbands had fought in the southern part of the country, and 593 families who had remained in North Vietnam and had no contact with Dioxin, showed that in the South the number of inborn anomalies was 15 times higher and the number of miscarriages and premature births respectively 1.5 and 3.3 times above the figures for North Vietnam.

According to data supplied by a gynaecological hospital in Ho Chi Minh City, the number of miscarriages in 1952 stood at 0.45 per cent, and from 1976 to 1979 retained the 11.20 per cent level. In this city the registered number of liver cancer patients increased 3.2 times as against the prewar period.

Scientists have noted that the character of changes affecting the genetic apparatus of Vietnamese who had come into contact with Agent Orange and Dioxin has much in common with the chromosomal disturbances observed among the victims of the A-bombings in Hiroshima and Nagasaki. There are two large population groups in the world today suffering from chromosomal disturbances: the survivors of the A-bombings of Nagasaki and Hiroshima in Japan, and the victims of Agent

Orange and Dioxin in Vietnam. The crimes perpetrated by the US Armed Forces are responsible for the suffering of both these groups.

Victims of conventional weapons, from the bayonet to the high-explosive bombs, were injured or maimed in action. Their physical sufferings were all their own and were not extended to their progeny. The use of nuclear and chemical weapons affecting as they do the hereditary apparatus of the survivors of nuclear bombings and chemical attacks, has given rise to a new category of victims, one embracing their children, grandchildren and succeeding generations of their offspring. This is one aspect of the inhuman nature of mass destruction weapons whose banning is insisted on by the peace forces the world over.

The production of chemical weapons holds no less dangerous prospects in store for people and their environment. Here are a few examples. The Dutch firm Philips-Duphar specialising in the manufacture of toxic agents has set up a large number of chemical waste dumps in the marshy areas situated only 5 miles from Amsterdam. Thousands of tons of diverse harmful agents have piled up at these dumps, being among them Dioxin and the salts of heavy metals. And it is not by chance that of late cases of cattle sterility and poultry epizooty have increased in this area.

In 1963 during the explosion of a chemical reactor at one of the Philips-Duphar plants in Amsterdam manufacturing Agent Orange for the US Army, a toxic mass containing Dioxin was ejected into the production shop and the plant's premises. Twenty workers from this shop and the inspectors investigating the causes of the explosion began to suffer from chlorance, a skin inflammation characteristic of Dioxin poisoning. Three workers and an employee of the Philips-Duphar firm died two years later from lethal doses of Dioxin. The plant was closed down.

In the earlier months after the explosion the firm's administration set its hopes on the natural ventilation of the premises and their decontamination. Toxicological control was carried out with the use of test animals. The animals died or were affected with disease upon inhaling the pollutant or coming into contact with contaminated objects. It was reported that the walls of the shop were contaminated to a level exceeding permissible norms billions of times: each kilogram of plaster contained up to a gram of Dioxin. The floor of the shop was to all appearances contaminated even more.

To decontaminate the shop, the plants administration hired 100 workers. The operation was carried out from March to July 1963. Detergents and different alkaline solutions were continuously used along with great amounts of water to wash the walls of the shop. The effect fell short of expectations. At the same time the washing procedure carried off some of the Dioxin into the sewage system leading to its contamination. Of the 44 workers taking part in the decontamination process who were examined in March 1964, 26 were suffering from chlorance. By 1977 all the 27 workers who had remained at the plant had specific skin disease typical of Dioxin poisoning.

The Philips-Duphar firm was compelled to destroy the plant. The debris along with a part of the equipment and soil with a total weight of nearly 1,000 tons was loaded on three barges and sunk in the vicinity of the Azores in the Atlantic.

Fourteen years later, in July 1976, a similar disaster took place near Seveso (20 kilometres north of Milan in Italy), when a chemical reactor exploded at one of the chemical enterprises of the Swiss firm Givaudan F. HofimannLa Roche Co., sending large amounts of Dioxin into the atmosphere. It contaminated a densely populated area of some 20 sq. km. with a population of 38,000. Ten days went by before Dioxin was discovered in samples of soil and vegetation and work was begun to localise the contaminated area and help the population. By the end of July the evacuation of the entire population from the zone with the highest contamination was completed.

All in all 77,000 animals, mostly rabbits, either perished or were destroyed for sanitary reasons. The high contamination zone was declared a no-man's land. In the less contaminated areas crop and animal farming had to be suspended. The upper layers of soil were removed and replaced by soil brought from other areas. The contaminated refuse and soil from the danger zone were buried in an 85,000 cu m concrete and plastic vault. Further examination of the area showed that although the land was ploughed up, the concentration of Dioxin in the soil was falling at an exceedingly slow rate. This poison was discovered in clinical materials taken from people who had remained in the zone during the first few weeks after the explosion.

To avoid deformities in newborn babies and different malfunctions in pregnant women, abortions were recommended to all expectant mothers living in the affected zone—an exceptional decision for a country with a mostly Catholic populations.

And here are a few examples from the experience of the USA. The Niagara River with its famous falls marks the state border between the USA and Canada. The US city of Niagara Falls lie on the right bank of the Niagara River and has a population of 77,000. A few years ago it turned out that some of the city's districts were situated on ground covering a huge pool of water containing toxic chemical refuse, including Dioxin. The discovery was prompted by numerous cases of cattle murrain and the perishing of birds and animals. Investigations led specialists to connect the increasing number of miscarriage and in-born deformities in the area with its possible contamination. It was established that out of the 36 examined citizens, 11 had numerous chromosomal aberrations. Mass evacuations were begun from districts with a high contact of Dioxin and other toxic agents in the waste products of local chemical industries. Houses were put up for sale. Selective soil tests showed that toxic agents had penetrated the subsoil waters and were threatening to poison the Niagara and Lake Ontario with all the ensuing unpredictable consequences.

Upon investigating the activities of the local chemical companies the New York State authorities found out that several dumps were sited within city limits, the biggest of them being in the Love Canal and Hyde Park districts.

At the end of the last century one William Love began building a canal between the Higher and Lower Niagara River. Although the work was later suspended he had succeeded in completing a one kilometre long and over 30 metre wide lake. The project remained unfinished. The open part of the canal, fed by the waters of the lake, had for many years supplied water to the swimming pools of Niagara Falls. In 1966 local residents began the construction of dams on the canal which divided the canal into several sections.

At the height of its production beam in manufacturing 2, 4, 5-T (a component of Agent Orange) the Hooker Chemical and Plastics Corporation began to dump production wastes in the Love Canal in the south-eastern part of the city. Company data testifies that 21,800 tons of chemical waste containing up 200 diverse chemical compounds including Dioxin and trichlorophenol were dumped in the canal waters. The most modest assessment sets the content of Dioxin in this part of the canal at nothing less than 5 kg or 20 times the amount ejected into the atmosphere during the explosion at the chemical plant in Amsterdam.

A dismal record belongs to Occidental Chemical, a branch company of the Hooker Chemical. In the north-western part of the canal running through the Hyde Park district it dumped 80,000 tons of chemical wastes including approximately 2 tons of Dioxin and 200 tons of trichlorophenol–source material used for the spontaneous synthesis of Dioxin.

Of late charges have been brought against the Hooker Chemical and Occidental Chemical companies with demands to destroy the chemical waste products accumulated underground. The cost of decontamination work is expected to run into millions, and it will take years to complete. The residents of Love Canal and Hyde Park areas have brought private charges against the chemical companies to the sum of 14 million dollars. But can money compensate for the ruined health of those who had for years inhaled or consumed through food and water the poison produced by industries serving the needs of the chemical war in Vietnam?

Tourists arriving at the International Stapleton Airport in the popular resort city of Denver (Colorado) cannot fail to notice the kilometres long rows of barrels line up not far from the airfield. A high fence runs the length of the blocks of chemicals plants: this is the Rocky Mountains chemical arsenal of the US Army, and the barrels contain diverse toxic agents.

The Rocky Mountains arsenal was set up in 1942 when it incorporated two plants specialising in the production of lewisite and yperite. Between 1952 and 1954 another plant was put into operation for the production of sarin, a toxic nerve agent. The arsenal's dumps were stocked with chemical and biological weapons.

US authorities officially claim that the arsenal's chemical plants have been mothballed since 1967. In its time the Shell Oil firm had contributed to the activities of these military chemical enterprises. On agreement with the US Army it had used the yperite plants facilities for the products were also interred in its territory. The Rocky Mountains arsenal covers an area of 7,000 hectares which begins within Denver's boundaries near the city's business sections.

According to the official version, in the early 1970s but actually long before that, birds stopping on the lakes located in the arsenal's territory for a respite during their migatory flights began to perish in large numbers. It was reported that chemical analyses had shown that the entire territory was contaminated by arsenic and mercury (the result of the former lewisite production), products resulting from chlorination and oxidation of yperite and its polysulphide compounds (residue left after distillation of yperite), chlorinated phenols and Dioxin (the result of Shell Oil production of Agent Orange), as well as toxic substances yielded during the production of Sarin.

In 1976, the US Department of Defence found it profitable to start preparations for closing down several chemical arsenals with the view of turning chemical weapons production over to private industry. The Rocky Mountains arsenal was declared to be the main project whose territories would be prepared for their contemplated transition for private needs. The first round of measures to clear its territory envisaged tearing down buildings and eliminating the interred waste products, or removing the upper soil layers on an area exceeding 1,000 hectares, and carting off for interment elsewhere of 12 million cubic metres of contaminated debris and soil. The cost of this first round of measures envisaged for the next 15 years was estimated at 357 million dollars, and that of the entire operation at 1,800 million dollars.

The decontamination of subsoil waters in the arsenal's territory and the adjoining areas poses a special problem. The waste products cast off into cesspools and lakes have penetrated subsoil waters and toxic agents have been discovered in wells drilled outside the arsenal's territory "Water taken from these wells has poisoned animals. Contaminated by Agent Orange' it destroys all vegetation and hence cannot be used even for watering crops".

The Colorado State authorities have brought charges against the US Department of the Army and Shell Oil. The defendants are now negotiating on how they will share the compensation for damages. To reassure the public the US Army and Shell Oil have of their own accord built three water purification plants along the perimeter of the territory which shed partially purified water into the city sewage system. This is, however, a purely symbolic gesture. Toxic wastes have penetrated the subsoil water carrying layers to an extent that is beyond exact assessment. For hundreds of years, or may be more, toxic wastes will remain in the Denver resort.

These facts refer only to a small part of US territory contaminated by agents dangerous to man and nature. These areas, known as they to the public, can be compared to the insignificant, visible part of a floating iceberg. Its greater invisible part can be identified with the territories of all the US military chemical arsenals and plants, chemical weapons depots, proving and exercise grounds where toxic agents are employed without exception.

Scientists have not yet fully assessed the potential danger for man and his environment of toxic wastes formed in the process of destroying stockpiles of toxic agents. This concerns the solutions containing decontamination products and the remains of toxic agents which are produced in huge quantities during the chemical neutralisation of toxic agents. As a rule the decontamination of every 10,000 tons of sarin yields 250,000-300,000 tons of dangerous waste. Decontamination of yperite produces 3-5 times more liquid waste products. In what way does the Pentagon intend to inter the waste products synthesized in the process of destroying toxic agents? In the 1960s attempts were made in the Rocky Mountains arsenal to pump such wastes into deep wells, an experiment leading to earthquakes in Denver. There is eloquent evidence that the Pentagon continues to dump toxic wastes into the gulf of Mexico and the Atlantic waters off the north-eastern coast of the USA.

This study confirms the conclusions highlighted by us in one of the chapters earlier about the impact of Use of Chemical and Biological Weapons during the Gulf War.

What is relevant is that almost two decades after the use of chemical and biological weapons in Vietnam, the same tragic story was repeated during the Gulf War. However, it is of far reaching importance in this connection, certain findings of the report on US Chemical and Biological Warfare related dual use export to Iraq from the United States.

We have already mentioned earlier how thousands of American servicemen and women are reportedly suffering from memory loss, muscle and joint pain, intestinal and heart problems, fatigue, rashes, sores, and running noses as a result of their service in the Gulf War. A number of veterans who have exhibited these symptoms since returning from the Gulf War reportedly have died. Members of their immediate families are now beginning to fall victim to some of the illnesses. Physicians have been unable to diagnose or treat the cause of the disorders.

There is substantial evidence supporting claims that US servicemen and women were exposed to low-level chemical warfare agents and possibly biological agents and toxins from a variety of sources. This exposure may account for many of the Gulf War illness symptoms. However, little is known about the long term consequences of exposure to low levels of nerve gas, although most are known to have cumulative toxic effects.

Even less is known about complications which might arise from exposure to combined agents and combined agent weapons. The combined agent strategy is intended to frustrate efforts at diagnosing these illnesses. Non-lethal exposure to pesticides can result in memory loss, and nerve agents are chemically related to pesticides. Many of the veterans complaining of Gulf War Syndrome illnesses suffer from among other disorders, memory loss. Many of the identified chemical and biological agents interfere with the body's neurotransmission possess, affecting the regulation of acetylcholine, neurotoxin acetylcholine, and other necessary enzymes required by nearly every physiological process. In order to detect irregularities such as those which might be caused by exposure to nerve gas, computer-read electro-encephalograms are needed. A physician probably would not be able to recognize the abnormalities through a visual EEG interpretation.

If biotoxins or biological agents were used or released in the Gulf War, detection requires that physicians and scientists have some idea of what they are looking for. Further, if mycotoxins (fungal toxins) or viruses were used or released they would be difficult to detect without the aid of advanced laboratory screening methods.

Non-lethal exposure to chemical warfare agents, some biological agents, mixed chemical/biotoxin agents and the administration of nerve agent pretreatment drugs could explain many of the symptoms of the Gulf War illness, as well as the inability to diagnose the disorders. Other possible causes for Gulf War syndrome have been suggested, such as exposure to pesticides, petrochemicals, burning of landfills and oil wells, depleted uranium from anti-tank munitions, or exposure to other environmental hazards.[1]

This candid admission by a committee of the Senate of the United States leads one to the conclusion that these biological and chemical weapons, for that matter nuclear weapons, have no geographical or regional boundaries. Nor do these weapons of mass destruction discriminate among race caste, colour, religion and creed. Their victims are human beings, irrespective of the fact whether they belong to the armed forces or civilians. There is something more to it.

The entire humanity on our planet when the 21st century is about to begin is perched on the brink of a precipice. Either the political elite, particularly those who have monopolised these weapons and are engaged in the dangerous game of proliferation of these weapons destroy them lock, stock and barrel or the humanity is pushed towards a disaster. This is the stark reality. The ideologues, the theoreticians and strategists are busy in spinning various theories. But this is only a mask. Beneath the surface is the ambition of certain powers to impose their politico-economic system, on other countries with a view to create an international order which serves the interests of the ruling elite of their countries. This is the crux of the problem. There is only one option: these Weapons should be destroyed at any cost otherwise these sophisticated weapons will surely destroy the mankind. It is in this context that the problems of Indian security should be seen within the global framework.

REFERENCE

1. A report of Chairman Donald W. Riegle, Jr. and Ranking Member Alfonse M-D'Amato of the Committee, on Banking, Housing and Urban Affairs with Respect to Export Administration, US Senate, p. 151, May 25, 1994.

11

Destruction of Weapons: Biological, Chemical and Nuclear

There is a theory that the universe was created as the result of a big bang. Now an artificial big bang, triggered by a wicked mind or a fatal error, threatens to turn the earth, the pearl of the universe, into a wasteland. The peril is extreme, for mankind's survival is at stake. The people of this earth must do everything in their power to safeguard life on our planet. The present generation, and not only that in one country, is responsible for the fate of civilisation and life on earth. It is this generation that will determine in the long run, whether the beginning of a new millennium in world history will be the latter's tragic epilogue or whether it will signal an inspiring prologue to the future.

Of course, the United States, Russia, Great Britain, China and France the world's greatest powers with far-reaching interests and immense material and intellectual potential, and possessing the overwhelming proportion of nuclear weapons, bear a special, one might even say unique responsibility before the international community for the fate of the world and its survival. Japan, which has already emerged as a super economic power with its stockpile of plutonium too holds a key positions, though officially it has not been declared a nuclear power. However, one cannot ignore the fact that it has all the potentials of becoming a nuclear power. Above all most of these countries still have huge stockpiles of biological and chemical weapons, notwithstanding the "Convention on the Prohibition of the Development, Production and Stockpiling of Bacteriological and Toxic Weapons and on the Destruction" better known as the Biological and Toxic Weapons Convention of 1972 and Chemical Weapons Convention of 1996.

Though it is not in the scope of this study to critically examine Nuclear Proliferation Treaty and Comprehensive Test Ban Treaty (NPT and CTBT), to create a world without weapons of mass destruction, all these four regimes should be taken in totality. In the final analysis it is the most developed nations which possess their stockpiles. Seen in this context, the people on this earth expect that all these countries, the United States in particular will display the wisdom, skill, responsibility and respect for the developing and underdeveloped countries to evolve a mechanism to create a new international order, a non-violent world without weapons of mass destruction.

However, it goes without saying that the existing regimes of NPT and CTBT are discriminatory because the members of the so-called Nuclear Club who also virtually monopolise the scientific knowhow of biological and chemical weapons are not at the moment in a mood to take a realistic stand. This is confirmed by their response to the nuclear tests by India and Pakistan in May 1998.

'Socialist System': Not Relevant Today

The Soviet Union has disintegrated for reasons into which one need not go in this study. The socialist system in East Europe has collapsed at least temporarily. China has embarked on a new path of economic reconstruction, what is now described as socialist market economy. Vietnam too has introduced basic economic reforms. Above all the relations between the US and China have already entered a new phase. Washington no longer considers Beijing as its enemy. On the contrary it has given China the status of the most favoured nation. After the merger of Hong Kong with China, China-Japan relations are likely to get a new boost. All these facts are being mentioned to make out that the old theory of a 'Communist Menace' has become irrelevant. That being the position, now a new theory has been evolved which is said to be about 'Civilisational Conflicts'. This concept too is a mask to cover the hard base of the new reality, the geoeconomic and geopolitical interests of the developed nations, including the old colonisers. The US with its hegemonistic ambitions stands in the forefront with a view to re-establish its leadership over the world. This leadership of course is now being challenged. There has been an erosion both in its authority and its ambitions. New contenders for the leadership have emerged including some of those who are members of the Nuclear Club. There are others who are not members of the Nuclear Club such as Japan. They too are competing in this struggle for leadership though in the typical characteristic of the Japanese, it is working on a low profile.

Asia Pacific Region: Centre of World Power

Both in terms of geopolitics and geoeconomics, Asia Pacific region in the 21st century will become a key factor. Seen in this context the political elite, economists and social scientists cannot afford to ignore the fast changing development in this region that too in a period of globalisation of economy and interdependence.

The centre of gravity of world power is steadily shifting from Europe to Asia-Pacific. Four countries USA, China, Japan and Russia, out of possibly about six including European Union (EU) or Germany and France, current major global powers are located here. India too has the potential of becoming an important force. Out of seven nations or state systems that may emerge as major players in the world in the next century, six are likely to be from this region—USA, China, Japan, Russia, ASEAN, or South East Asia, India and the EU.

The rise of the Asia-Pacific as the centre of world power has been generally measured in economic terms with main focus on East Asia. Gross Domestic Product (GDP) growth rates in East Asia on an average was twice that of the other regions till the recent financial crisis in some of the ASEAN countries. At this rate, by early in the next century, quite probably five of the six largest economies in the world may be in the Asia-Pacific region—Greater China, USA, Japan, ASEAN, and India.

That is the reason that this region has been described as the region of tomorrow. This is true both literally and metaphorically.

The hard base of the reality is that under the cover of either "Civilisational Conflicts" or danger to the "International stability" by regional conflicts or both these factor are being used to justify the theory of military deterrence. Behind this, there are two basic factors which are operating; a recession and growing unemployment in the developed nations. These problems can only be solved by penetrating into the economies of the Asia Pacific region where two-thirds of the population of our planet live.

Secondly, the military complexes including manufactures of military hardware need a new market. This market is only available in this region.

That also explains partly how some of the countries of this region are being encouraged to purchase military hardware including the most sophisticated weapons as has been mentioned earlier.

Thus new images of threat to stability are being fabricated. This is the main bottleneck of the vicious circle to which this region is being pushed. We have already examined in this study how Iraq was given full support, raw material and technology to manufacture biological and chemical weapons, with a view to drive a permanent wedge between Iran and Iraq. But when Iraq did not fall in line, it was singled out and heavy sanctions were imposed on it, though some other countries in the region had and continue to have chemical and biological weapons as we have mentioned in this study earlier. This implies that this vicious circle can only be broken by re-awakening a new awareness among the people of the world as a whole. This is indeed a challenging task. Nevertheless, it is better to raise a feeble voice rather than as a passive spectator at the new tragedy which is in the offing.

We have delved briefly into past history to try and understand how the world arrived at its current critical stage and the imminent peril to human race weapons of mass destruction, nuclear weapons in particular.

According to M. Halperin, a prominent US expert in arms control and Director of the Centre of Studies for National Security for several decades, the US Military doctrine has rested on the dangerous assumption, erroneous in the extreme, of the possibility of waging and winning a nuclear war. According to him, combat nuclear devices of any type are not a weapon in the usual meaning of the word. No belligerent can employ them as a means of warfare to achieve victory. Should these weapons be used, they would spell the death of the enemy, the attacker and all of civilisation. There can be no victors in such a war. In the last two years of the present century, strategic experts throughout the world now seem to have come to the conclusion that weapons of mass destruction, nuclear weapons in particular, are increasingly becoming either as weapons of "deterrence" or as weapons of "political bargaining".

A mere list of their post-war military doctrines and strategic concepts provides ample proof that power politics has always been the focal point in Washington's ideas of "national security".

While the ruins of Hiroshima and Nagasaki were still emitting their deadly radiation, the US adopted the "massive retaliation strategy". It was based on the US nuclear monopoly, impunity, and omnipotence, stemming from the conviction that North America was totally invulnerable to any attack. It did not last long. Soon thereafter the US nuclear monopoly was broken. The 1957 launching of the first Soviet artificial earth satellite impelled the US military and political leaders to modify their plans. Even Washington's die-hards became painfully aware that in case of a military conflict the United States could become the target of a sizeable counterstrike. This led to the flexible response strategy in the 1960s, which of necessity took note of the approximate parity between the strategic arsenals of the USSR and of the USA, known as the nuclear stalemate. The new strategy provided for graduated use of military force, whose amount would be commensurate with the scale of the new threat. This graduated response also provided for the preparation for and conduct of any war—world or local, nuclear or conventional, big or small. This meant that the massive retaliation strategy was not completely abandoned, as the US Administration claimed, but became part and parcel of the flexible response strategy which replaced it.

Throughout the last 50 years the Pentagon's military thinking and specific strategic plans have been repeatedly updated. Michio Kaku and Daniel Axelrod who authored *To Win a Nuclear War: The Pentagon Secret War Plans*, published in 1987, point out that an attentive reading of the Pentagon documents shows that contrary to the official commitment to deterrence and defence, in reality the US Department of Defence was thinking in terms of using nuclear weapons in order to threaten the enemy with nuclear war, wage such a war, survive and even win a nuclear war. This thinking was embodied in the atomic diplomacy of Truman's time, balancing on the brink of war in the days of Eisenhower-Dulles, the controlled escalation and flexible response of the McNamara years, limited nuclear options of the Nixon vintage and the waging of nuclear war, doctrine of the Carter years, which clearly shows that its authors thought that such a war could be fought and won. The book also follows the evolution of the supremacy at all levels of conflict, a concept underlying the post-war US military doctrines.

According to a White House report dated 28 January 1987 the national security strategy, the global objectives, and the very nature of the menace demand that the country be prepared to defend its interests at frontiers as remote as possible from the United States. Following this line, the national strategy prominently features forward-based systems, backed up by strong military alliances. The report went on to say that in order to maintain this relationship the United States would continue to maintain large peace time land, sea, and air forces at bases, in Europe, the Atlantic and the Pacific, as well as in the Western Hemisphere and in the Indian Ocean.

Obviously the Pentagon based its strategic concepts on the fallacious idea that national security can be enhanced through military build-up and the creation of new weapon systems. It continues to count on advances in military technology and still supports the dangerous philosophy of nuclear deterrence.

Certain West European political notables, such as Margaret Thatcher, Jacques Chirac and Helmut Kohl, also claim that the idea of a nuclear-free world is utopian and that nuclear weapons are a powerful factor of deterrence. There are others who sincerely believe that the nuclear evil is necessary to prevent the even greater evil of war.

Surely, it is obvious that the nuclear safeguard is not wholly fool-proof. The greater the nuclear stockpiles the greater the chances of unpleasant surprises.

There have appeared new, previously unknown risk factors. Foremost among them is that of an accidental, unplanned nuclear catastrophe. It is considerably magnified by the time factor, when split-second decisions must be made. This has led to employing increasingly intricate computerised devices. This engenders the devolution of political decision-making to robots, which are far from being perfect and fool-proof. Even the most advanced equipment is no guarantee against a fatal miscalculation or error.

This risk has been acknowledged by sober minded people in the United States. For example, former Deputy Attorney General John W. Douglas wrote in *The New York Times:* "We are approaching a hair-trigger environment. We would do well to remember that in the past, with few exceptions, man has utilized every weapon he has invented. And plainly the risk of nuclear conflict is growing. Technical changes and national strategies are magnifying the chances for fatal miscalculations. Reaction times have been cut, nuclear weapons have been introduced to the battlefield, first-strike capabilities have been enhanced. Meanwhile, technological developments continue to undermine the capacity for rational decision-making in periods of superpower crisis."[1]

Prominent historian and diplomat George F. Kennan in 1987 spring issue of Foreign Affairs states: "It is entirely clear to me that Soviet leaders do not want a war with us and are not planning to initiate one. In particular, I have never believed that they have seen it as in their interests to over-run Western Europe militarily, or that they would have launched an attack on that region generally even if the so-called nuclear deterrent had not existed. I see the weapons race in which we and they are now involved as a serious threat in its own right, not because of aggressive intentions on either side but because of the compulsions, the suspicions, the anxieties such a competition engenders, and because of the very serious danger it carries with it of unintended complications—by error by computer failure, by misread signals, or by mischief deliberately perpetrated by third parties.[2]

Reagan's Strategic Defence Initiative was also the upshot of the deterrence philosophy. It was becoming plainer than ever that it was launched not to deter a non-existent aggressor and protect the USA against a mythical threat but to help in the implementation of the US imperial policies gripped in a deadlock because of strategic parity, and out of which the US Administration hoped to lead it with the help of space experiments. It is plain, for example, from a 1986 book by former National Security Advisor Zbigniew Bresesinski entitled *Game Plan.*[3] Its central idea is that military supremacy in space is becoming a mighty weapon in advancing one's geopolitical goals on earth. With the enormous destructive yield of nuclear weapons that could be used against earth targets, unchallenged reign in space could become even more vital than was control of the high seas. A country trying to stand up to the political demands of a power, enjoying overwhelming space superiority, would run the risk of a crushing blow and would be unable to retaliate. From this Brzesinski drew the following conclusion : the space race is fuelled by the desire to acquire strategic means of pressure.

In drawing up the ABM Treaty the USSR and the USA agreed that a large scale anti-missile defence system would destabilise the situation and increase the war risk. Such a system would be effective only against a counterstrike by the depleted nuclear forces of a nuclear attack victim. That is why a space shield is must for a country that plans to be the first to raise the nuclear sword. Kaku and Axelrod point out that even Star Wars weapons can never become an effective means of defence. The

ABM system has another potential application: even an imperfect, partial shield has an enormous military potential. A country possessing such a shield would be able to deliver the first strike, destroy most of the enemy's land based missiles and then use the shield to neutralise the weakened counterstrike. According to this scenario, the role of the sword will be played by MX, Trident and other missiles, which would destroy the enemy's rockets in their silos, and the Star Wars shield would intercept the remaining rockets surviving the first strike.

The Pentagon has admitted the possibility of hundreds and even thousands of warheads, with an unprecedented yield penetrating the US ABM defences. That is why they are designed primarily to protect the command and control structures, nuclear stockpiles, missile silos, nuclear reactors, etc.

Star Wars Programme

In December 1986 the President was given a new version of the Star Wars programme, calling for the deployment of the first echelon of a large-scale ABM system as early as 1994. The purpose of the project is to speed up the transition from the research stage to the deployment of space-based systems. The plan also calls for the orbiting of scores of spaceships armed with small rockets designed to strike at enemy warheads in midflight, as well as for creating a satellite-based system of intelligence and surveillance. The planned ABM defences would also include hundreds of land-based missiles. The system is designed to protect a limited number of military installations.

Having set its sights on achieving military superiority by means of a Star Wars programme, Washington tried to embroil the USSR in costly military space projects. American experts estimate that the development of an anti-ballistic defence system may prove to be 4 or 5 times more expensive than the development by the other side of missiles capable of penetrating it. Clearly mindful of the economic effects of a space arms race for the USSR Edward Teller, known as father of the American hydrogen bomb, declared that should the USSR follow the US example and start developing its own large-scale ABM space system, the SDI would be fully justified.

However, history proves that disarmament is an exceedingly difficult process. It is made even more difficult by the existence and ongoing modernisation of nuclear weapons and the use of the latest advances in science and technology to further whip up the arms race, on top of which stockpiles of biological and chemical weapons exist. Mankind has no option but to retreat from the nuclear abyss and find fundamentally new ways of securing the survival of our civilisations.

It took millions of years of evolution for living beings to appear on our planet. The nuclear and space age has placed it at the risk of instantaneous destruction. This is unthinkable. Scientists have found no evidence of the existence of rational beings on other planets of the solar system and even in the rest of the universe. So what could be nobler than to safeguard the survival of humankind.

The invention and stockpiling of weapons of mass destruction have brought the world close to the point of no return. Mankind is at a crossroads and as a result of the development and subsequent stockpiling beyond all reasonable bounds of nuclear weapons and their delivery vehicles man has become technically capable of terminating his own existence. The simultaneous accumulation of acute social problems in the world and attempts to tackle them forcefully using methods from the Stone Age, the problems of a fundamentally changed world make catastrophe highly likely in political terms as well. The militarisation of the mind and of the way of life weakens and even removes altogether any moral inhibitions with regard to nuclear suicide.

The fateful dilemma is this: either political thinking will be modified to match the categorical imperative of our time or civilisation and life itself on earth will perish. There is no other choice. Although the clash of ideologies will continue, the realities of the nuclear age call for new thinking, a new philosophy of world intercourse. Today security is no longer determined by the number of missiles, submarines or warplanes. War and armed forces can no longer be accepted as rational instruments of politics. Like a group of mountain climbers roped together, the nations of the world can either continue their efforts to scale the peak or plunge into the abyss together.

This is a military and political imperative, as much as is a moral one. In our complex and controversial world, a humanitarian largeness of thinking in statesmen and politicians should become proof of a new approach to contemporary issues. This largeness is no less necessary than the art of political astuteness, diplomatic caution and parliamentary oratory.

Life has made it imperative that they transcend narrowly-understood national interests and reorient their thinking towards the needs of mankind as a whole. Statesmen are thus responsible not only for the welfare and safety of their own people but also for the security and prosperity of the whole of humanity, because in present day conditions genuine national interests are identical to those of all people on earth. That is why now that the 20th century is drawing to a close there should be no mistrust, ill-feeling, alienation and enmity in relations among peoples. Ideological intolerance is dividing nations which is unacceptable.

The time has come to place the relationship between the developed and developing countries on a more solid foundation, without detriment to their own identity, their membership, their systems and alliances. All of these countries can play a positive role in efforts to stabilise the international situation and promote mankind's progress.

But time is running out and there is the mounting risk that weapons may get out of hand and become even more lethal. Diverse militarist programmes are afoot in the West, fuelled by nostalgia for the good old days. Many Western countries' policies still show a lack of responsibility and new thinking. It is still not understood that without the new thinking politics degrade into unpredictable improvisation, risk-ridden and not based on expendiency.

Philosophical heritage of mankind shows that ideas fraught with enormous consequences are always simple. So is the idea of ridding mankind of the millstone of nuclear weapons and weapons in general. Its implementation will be of immeasurable benefit to the peoples of the earth. It will put an end to tensions, mistrust and enmity, remove for ever the threat of annihilation of all living things, and last but not least, it will enable mankind to come to grips with global issues.

It is today that the foundations for the future are being laid, and we are duty-bound to preserve our unique civilisation and life on earth, to help reason to triumph over nuclear madness and to create the conditions for the harmonious development of humanity. The right to live in peace and freedom is a basic human right which must be guaranteed.

On the face of it, it may look as an unrealistic utopia. However, all the philosophies—religious, spiritual and political—place human beings and their well being as the driving force of history. Once the ideas, as Jawaharlal Nehru once said, grip the minds of the people they become a material force of change. This shows if humanity has to be saved from destruction, the common people should be roused and mobilized to hold back the hands of those who are perpetrators of violence through stockpiles of nuclear, biological and chemical weapons. There is neither any shortcut to this alternative nor any other option.

REFERENCES

1. *The New York Times*, September 29, 1986.
2. *Foreign Affairs*, Spring 1987, pp. 888-89.
3. Z. Brzezinski, Game Plan: A Geostrategic Framework for the Conduct of the US-Soviet Contest, Boston, New York, 1986.

12

Relevance of Nehru's Vision for Humanism and Non-Violent World Order

Diethelm Weidemann

In this short paper the well-known Czechoslovak scholar has analysed how Nehru's vision of world without weapons of mass destruction can be built on the basis of humanism, equality, respect for the sovereignty of all the nations–big or small developed or underdeveloped. It is on the basis of this world outlook that he evolved India's foreign policy and took one initiative after another to translate this into a reality. It is this policy through which India carved out a unique place in the international community. This enabled India to follow an independent foreign policy and in the process set an example before all the newly liberated countries. Again it was precisely this policy which made it possible for India to resist all foreign pressures. Though the author has not dealt with the central question of building India's defence potential, anyone who makes on objective assessment of development of India's economic base, technology and updating of India's armed forces would agree that Nehru's thought structures relating to both these aspects—foreign policy and internal developments—are relevant today.

Jawaharlal Nehru's death anniversary falls on 27th May. The hands of death snatched him away from the Indian people and humanity on this day in 1964. It left a great void, which nearly thirty four years since his death has not succeeded in filling. On the contrary, the greatness and uniqueness of what Nehru had accomplished has become more and more evident with every passing year. The year 1989 was also the year which people throughout the world observed as the birth centenary of Nehru remembering his life and work with great respect and admiration. However, his vision for humanism and world peace was never so relevant as it is today.

Nehru's Contribution

Nehru was a brilliant figure of the twentieth-century. From the late 1920s until his death, he exerted an extraordinary influence on the theory and practice of Indian constitution and his country's economic, domestic and foreign policies. To the development of Indian society he added important elements related to its future and others of a humanitarian character—basic principles of national formation and consolidation, which have remained alive to this very day and are likely to continue to be so for a very long time yet.[1]

A generally recognized national politician and defender of India's sovereign interests, he was a statesman of enormous international stature. In this century, which has been shaken by war, crisis and conflict, he was one of the first to reject the idea of war as an instrument of politics and to regard the arrival of weapons of mass destruction, biological, chemical and nuclear weapons as posing the ultimate threat to human survival.

In 1927, he began making crucial contributions to the stand taken by the Indian National Congress on issues of international importance. All the important maxims of India's later foreign policy with the exception of non-alignment[2] were developed under his influence in the period from 1927 to 1936.[3] These may be summarized in this way:

(i) India should pursue a foreign policy based on independence and equality.

(ii) In its foreign policy India should be unrelenting in its condemnation of imperialism and colonialism.

(iii) India should show solidarity and give support, to other nations in their struggle for freedom, a struggle that constituted a general international process.

(iv) India's foreign policy should mainly aim to encourage peace, which would be achieved by the establishment of peaceful relations with all countries.

(v) India should condemn every kind of war and refuse to take part in imperialist wars.[4]

These maxims, which embodied a clear anti-colonialist stance, an uncompromising denunciation of fascism, and a consistent refusal to connive at expansion, aggression and war, had already stood the test of history when the Second World War broke out, as I have clearly demonstrated elsewhere.[5]

In 1946, Nehru again became the dominant figure in every sphere of Indian foreign policy. His maxims and his international reputation won India its place in world politics and enabled it to pursue a foreign policy that was of supraregional importance.

In acknowledging Nehru's contribution, we may easily be trapped by a desire to reflect on, and describe, nothing but India's foreign policy itself. This would not, however, allow an adequate appraisal of the historical significance of Nehru's efforts in the context of this policy.

The first and most fundamental aspect of these was his basic approach to foreign policy matters, which was radically different from the approach dictated by traditional bourgeois views and the pragmatic attempts made by many developing countries in an effort to find their bearings in the maze of international affairs.

Nehru regarded the world and mankind as a unified whole. He believed that all people and countries, which had jointly inherited world civilization, shared the same obligation of preserving that civilisation.[6] This idea determined all the basic principles that he was seeking to pursue in Indian foreign policy.

Throughout his life, he was a committed and powerful defender of India's legitimate national interests. He was absolutely convinced that a country should never pursue its own national interests at the expense of those of other countries and peoples. He has resolutely opposed to any kind of foreign policy dictated solely by emotion. Yet though his approach was profoundly rational, it did not lack passion. This was shown by the shock and disappointment he felt after the outbreak of the Sino-Indian conflict. The rationality of his attitude was illustrated by the fact that he categorically refused to make concessions to prejudice and expediency, for example, when taking decisions on how to vote at the United Nations. In 1947 he gave the Indian UN delegation a clear instruction that it should judge every issue solely on its merits.[7]

Another important element of his foreign policy was that he attached a great deal of importance to a proper relationship being observed between means and ends; in other words, his own understanding of humanism, ethics, morality and democracy made him demand most emphatically that the choice of means should always be appropriate to the desired end, in foreign policy just as much as in any other fields of politics.[8]

Nehru arrived at his foreign policy maxims on the basis of his principled attitude towards international developments, of his belief in the indissoluble oneness of the world and of mankind—a belief that he shared with Sarvepalli Radhakrishnan, that brilliant philosopher and one-time President of India,[9] and of his ability to make a proper assessment of the role that he assigned to peace in these maxims became visible as early as the late 1920s and early 1950s.[10] The lessons taught by the second world war and the arrival of nuclear arms reinforced Nehru's belief that peace should be more than just a hope because it was "an emergent necessity."[11] N.S. Rajan was, therefore, right when he said that "the primary and overriding goal of India's foreign policy under Nehru was maintenance of international peace and security."[12] As a result, the governing Indian National Congress in 1943 defined the principal aims of India's foreign policy as "the promotion of world peace, the freedom of all nations, racial equality, and the ending of imperialism and colonialism."[13]

In Nehru's eyes, peace was the top priority in three important ways :

(i) He regarded peace as the basic condition for fruitful relations between peoples and countries. He defined it not only as the mere absence of war, but also as a way of living, thinking and acting[14] and as a state of society that could only be achieved through the creation of a climate of peace.[15]

(ii) He saw peace as an indispensable external condition for national development, especially for economic and social progress.

(iii) He believed that Hiroshima had made peace imperative because, from then on, the very existence of mankind was under threat a fact that was due to the development of a new kind of weaponry—nuclear arms.

It must be emphasized again and again that Nehru was, from the very beginning, one of those politicians who constantly struck a warning note in their utterances. He said that the choice today in this nuclear age is one of utter annihilation and destruction of civilisation or of some way to have peaceful coexistence between nations.[16] He concluded that another world war will spell ruin, and we shall not escape the general disaster. We are determined to make every possible effort in the cause of peace. That explains our present foreign policy.[17] He was firmly convinced that there would be either constructive international cooperation and the preservation of the values of world civilization or an end to civilization generally, an end to mankind.[18]

It is no exaggeration to say that Nehru's view of peace anticipated what is today known throughout the world as the new thinking.[19] Closely associated with it was his general rejection of war as an instrument of politics, an idea reflected in all the Indian National Congress (INC's) foreign policy resolutions initiated by him from 1927. It was an important element in the INC's attitude towards the second world war, and part and parcel of India's foreign policy after 1947. The idea was also manifest in countless foreign policy statements[20] and the attitude of his successors—Lal Bahadur Shastri, Indira Gandhi and Rajiv Gandhi–towards war and aggression.

Nehru: As a Politician

Nehru's achievements as a politician were not the least reflected in the fact that he was one of the first of the unfortunately very few public figures in the formerly colonial world to realize that there were objective links between imperialism and war, imperialism and fascism, and imperialism and colonialism, and to understand that neo-colonialism was nothing but a form of colonial exploitation that was a little more subtle than what colonialism had previously been. The rebuff that he administered to the forces who represented such causes was very dramatic indeed.

To translate the above-mentioned maxims into practice, in other words, to ensure peace, abolish suppression, aggression and war, and establish equality among nations, Nehru favoured the policy of peaceful coexistence, considering it as the basis of any national foreign policy and a norm to be observed in all relations among peoples and countries.

Because of the acute international crisis which began in 1946, and of the confrontation brought about by the existence of opposing military alliances, he believed that non-alignment had to be the basic principle governing his country's international behaviour. I wish to state very clearly at this point that Nehru made it plain that India adopted this principle solely because it was interested in peace. He said: "The preservation of peace forms the central aim of India's policy. It is in the pursuit of this policy that we have chosen the path of non-alignment in any military or like pact or alliance".[21] I think I can spare myself the trouble of giving a detailed account of India's position on peaceful coexistence and non-alignment, because it is widely known and further explanation at this point would definitely go beyond the limits of the tribute I wish to pay to Nehru's life and work.

In his foreign policy concept, Nehru established a very direct link between the basic humanitarian and democratic aim of his policy and the question of the relationship between means and ends. Incidentally, it is in this connection that the philosophy of Mahatma Gandhi exercised clearly discernible direct influence on the theory and practice of Indian foreign policy. Nehru himself made this plain when he said: "We can never forget the great teaching of our Master that the ends do not justify the means. Perhaps most of the troubles in the world today are due to the fact that people have forgotten this basic doctrine and are prepared to justify any means in order to obtain their objectives".[22]

Some of the most important elements of Nehru's views can be summed up as follows :

(i) The primacy of law in both basic foreign policy conduct and the approach to settling all kinds of issues, clashes of interest, and conflicts;

(ii) The peaceful accommodation of interests, which should be the most important means of settling inter-governmental and international issues, with such settlements never being allowed to give rise to new difficulties;

(iii) The establishment of consensus, which is the kind of accommodation of interests that is most appropriate under the conditions prevailing in the world today;

(iv) The top priority of negotiations among the methods of foreign policy, since they are most appropriate in ensuring the primacy of law, the accommodation of interest, the establishment of consensus, and the pursuit of actual diplomacy.

All things considered, the question arises: what new elements did Nehru's basic approach, his basic principles, and his views on the proper relationship between means and ends introduce into India's foreign policy and in consequence, into international politics? Let us try to outline these elements under four headings :

(i) Nehru's approach to global issues corresponded, to a considerable extent, with the completely new requirements that had arisen after the second world war. It served to ensure peace and the security of nations. His ideas of the contradictory unity of the world, the top priority of peace (in the absence of any feasible alternative), and the inextricable links between peace and development have stood the test of time and are more important today than at any time before.[23]

(ii) Nehru's views on the relations between means and ends and on the methods to be employed in implementing India's foreign policy, which he defined very closely indeed, became part and parcel of the policy, behaviour, and decision-making processes of the movement of non-aligned countries, and were as a result turned into important factors in international politics.

In paying tribute to Jawaharlal Nehru, we remember a politician who, through his efforts in many fields, made an important contribution to opening up for his people the road to our present day, and gave millions in his country the vision of a future of peace, independence and social justice. We are honouring the memory of a man who worked indefatigably to create a world community in which the three ideals of humanitarianism, democracy and equality were supreme.

REFERENCES

1. Schaller, E., Weidemann. D, Zum 100,. Geburtstag Jawaharlal Nehru.
2. C.f. Nehru, J., *India's Foreign Policy, Selected Speeches*, September 1946 to April 1961, Delhi 1971, p. 2 ff.
3. See, inter alia, Nehru, J., The Psychology of Indian Nationalism In: *Selected Works of Jawaharlal Nehru*, Vol. 2, Delhi 1972, pp. 259-70.
4. *Jawaharlal Nehru: A Political Leader*, Prague 1974, pp. 63-104.
5. Jawaharlal Nehru, Indian National Movement and the Beginning of World War II. In: *GDR Review*, Berlin, No. 8/1989.
6. Cf. Nehru, India's Foreign Policy....., p. 2, 173-79.
7. Constituent Assembly (Legislative) Debates, Vol. 2, Delhi 1947, Cols 1259-64.
8. *The Hindu*, Madras, December 20, 1956.
9. Cf. Radhakrishnan, S, *Towards a New World.*, Delhi 1980.

10. See Indian National Congress, Madras 1927, Resolution VI, In: AICC–The Background of India's Foreign Policy, Delhi 1952, p. 47.
11. Lok Sabha Debates, Delhi, April 24, 1954, Col. 5581.
12. Rajan, M.S., *India's Foreign Relations during the Nehru Era: Some Studies*, Delhi 1976, p. xii.
13. AICC, Resolutions on Foreign Policy, Delhi 1957, p. 3.
14. *The Hindu*, October 21, 1954.
15. *Ibid.*, May 3, 1954.
16. *Jawaharlal Nehru's Speeches*, Vol. 4, September 1957, April 1964., Delhi 1964, p. 317.
17. *Ibid.*, Vol. 2, August 1949, February 1953, Delhi 1954, p. 5.
18. Cf. T.N. Kaul, A World Vision in the Nuclear Age. In: Haksar Nehru's Vision of Peace and Security in the Nuclear Age, Delhi 1987, pp. 79-83.
19. V.D. Chopra, goes as far as to establish a direct link. Cf. V.D. Chopra, Nehru and Gorbachev. In: *Ibid*, pp. 115-31.
20. Cf. Jawaharlal Nehru, India's Foreign Policy, pp. 187-91, 199-200, 203-206.
21. Jawaharlal Nehru's Speeches, Vol. 3, March 1953,-August 1957, Delhi 1958, p. 49.
22. *The Hindu*, January 24, 1954.
23. Cf. Government of India, Press and Information Bureau, Prime Minister Rajiv Gandhi's address to the Third Special Session on Disarmament of the United Nations General Assembly, June 9, 1988, Delhi 1988.

13

The Nehru Era and Foundations of India's Foreign Policy

Jawaharlal Nehru was one of the greatest captains of freedom struggle, a man who was next only to Gandhi in his contribution to the shaping of that struggle; he gave it a rational and modern basis, a secular and economic bias, and a truly international outlook. Then, for seventeen years, he was free India's first Prime Minister, and whatever the controversies over certain policies, it cannot be denied that he laid the foundations of our democracy, secularism, socialism, and policy towards the rest of the world. This record cannot be forgotten or wished away, and whatever else may happen, these unending processes which he established cannot be reversed. Even if policy makers may wish to reverse them, the people will not allow them to be reversed.

Jawaharlal Nehru had a high ambition for his people and always thought of being nearer to history than to office, and history has a right to assess him. What was the basis of his life, thinking, and actions? He was one of the most courageous of men, though he would not call himself the most courageous, one of the noblest of men, though he would not call himself the noblest, one of the most intelligent of men, though he would not call himself the most intelligent, and one of the most energetic of men, though he would not call himself the most energetic. He was a combination of all these and other qualities in a rare degree and he was thus one of the finest instruments of historical forces the world has known. In the days of the English Civil War, he may have been Cromwell leading his Ironsides; in the days of the American Revolution, he may have been a Jefferson indicting the Declaration of Independence and in the days of the Russian Revolution, he may have been a Lenin, not making much distinction between violence and non-violence. He would not have failed to respond with his resilience of mind and independence of spirit to any historical circumstances, but growing in Gandhi's India and in the context of the Indian Revolution, he was Jawaharlal Nehru. This Jawaharlal Nehru, the people loved from the early years of life and they did not want him to be any one else, and critics also criticised him for what he was forty years ago, thirty years ago, twenty years ago, or ten years ago, and still criticise him for not being someone else. But he could not be anyone else than what he was, and if he had grown harder or softer, he would have been someone different, not Jawaharlal Nehru.

Jawaharlal Nehru contained many men. No other great leader has ever combined such high seriousness and sense of purpose with such a spirit of adventure. He was no self-conscious artist who practised poetry or cultivated style; his art sprang from his pagan heart and an abundance of feeling combined with an acute intelligence; he did everything with style yet his style was that of a free spirit nursed in the rhythms of nature, the style of a man of action who was also a man of thought.

By whatever standards anyone can judge him, Jawaharlal Nehru's place is by the side of Gandhi. Like Buddha and Asoka, like Marx and Lenin, Gandhi and Jawaharlal Nehru go together. What else, besides? It is for history to worry.[1]

Nehru and India's Foreign Policy

The foreign policy of independent India is essentially a continuation of the "Nehruvian line" in external relations. This was shaped at the turn of the 20s and 30s and reflected the anti-imperialist mood of the Indian national movement. An inseparable part of Nehru's world outlook, and particularly his attitude to international problems, was his determined opposition to India's participation in imperialist war and, for that matter, in any war. This attitude became the basic tenet of a resolution adopted by the Indian National Congress (INC) at the end of 1927, the first resolution in fact in which the fundamentals of the party's approach to international relations began to crystallize. The abhorrence of violent methods in the settlement of conflicts has since been an inseparable part of the political philosophy of the INC.

The essential principles of the foreign policy of independent India were defined by Jawaharlal Nehru when, as head of the Interim Government in 1946, he made his famous radio broadcast from Delhi on 7 September.

He expressed the determination of his government to keep away from the power blocs or groups aligned against one another which have led in the past to world wars and which may again lead to disasters on an even vaster scale.

The peaceful approach adopted by Nehru was intended to secure the vital national interests of India, above all its independent political, social and economic development. In his view, peace and freedom are indivisible and the denial of freedom anywhere must endanger freedom elsewhere and lead to conflict and war. Mutual collaboration in the interests of strengthening peace and freedom was therefore an urgent task for all liberated nations.

In a broadcast from London on 12 January, 1951, Nehru expressed his attitude towards the problem of war and peace in these terms: "what we need is a passion for peace and for civilized behaviour in international affairs....If we desire peace, we must develop the temper of peace and try to win even those who may be suspicious of us or who think they are against us....we cannot seek peace in the language of war or of threats".

Nehru's conception was based on the assumption that peace could not be promoted by creating positions of strength. In the nuclear age, every effort by a nation state to increase its own strength at the expense of others threatened to disturb the global power balance culminating in humanity's self-destruction. Nehru firmly believed that entering into military alliances and establishing military bases in foreign territories accentuated discord and increased the possibility of a military conflict. There was no alternative to the peaceful approach though it could not absolutely guarantee peace, since violence created more problems than it could solve. The only way to settle the differences was through negotiation, mutual concessions and accommodation.

Such an understanding of international relations closely followed the ideal of tolerance and peaceful reconciliation of opposing viewpoints which is considered one of the traditional Indian values. Solving controversial issues through negotiations was by no means a new or original method, but if applied by a non-aligned state like India, which was not one of the parties to the conflict, it could help adversaries to reach a compromise. The essence of India's approach in such negotiations was that neither party should suffer a significant loss and that it was necessary to utilize whatever common ground existed and which was favourable to reconciliation. As an example of the application of such a policy we may cite the efforts of Indian diplomacy to have the People's Republic of China admitted to the UNO and to achieve negotiated settlements on Indochina and Suez.

The leaders of independent India were of the opinion that the best method of achieving security was a positive policy of friendship with other countries. As Indira Gandhi said at a seminar in New Delhi on 31 August 1970: "It is possible through friendship to out manoeuvre hostility." Consequently India has always made every effort to develop multilateral international collaboration and friendly relations among countries with different social systems.

It was to the problems of disarmament, and particularly nuclear disarmament, that Indian diplomacy always devoted particular attention. Influenced by the tragic fate of Hiroshima and Nagasaki, which were virtually obliterated by United States' nuclear bombing in 1945, Gandhi argued: "The moral to be legitimately drawn from the supreme tragedy of the bomb is that it will not be destroyed by counter-bombs even as violence cannot be by counter-violence".

In 1953, the UN General Assembly adopted an Indian resolution which affirmed the world body's earnest desire for the elimination and prohibition of atomic, hydrogen, bacterial, chemical and other weapons of war and mass destruction and for the attainment of these ends through effective means. In April 1954 Nehru, by then India's Prime Minister, reacted to the American hydrogen bomb test on Bikini Atoll with an urgent appeal to stop nuclear testing and start negotiations immediately on an agreement which would end the production and stockpiling of such weapons. This was the first concrete attempt by the non-aligned countries, in whose name Nehru was speaking to secure an immediate suspension of nuclear weapon tests. It led to India and other neutral states taking the lead in the general effort to prevent humanity from sliding to the brink of the nuclear precipice.

Non-Aligned Movement and India's Role

India has been taking the lead among the member countries of the non-aligned movement in calling upon the international community to outlaw the threat of use of nuclear weapons to negotiate a comprehensive nuclear test ban treaty, to restrict the production of nuclear weapons and fissionable materials for military purposes, and to prevent the development, production and dissemination of all kinds of weapons of mass destruction.

India made a positive contribution to the effort to mobilise world public opinion for disarmament and the halting of the arms race, which had reached frenzied proportions, by issuing an appeal on 22 May 1984—together with Argentina, Mexico, Greece, Sweden and Tanzania—to the five nuclear powers. These proposals urged world recognition of the need for nuclear disarmament and were further developed in a declaration adopted at the meeting of the Delhi Six in the Indian capital on 28 January 1985. This initiative by Rajiv Gandhi, who was then developing India's policy on weapons of mass destruction, particularly nuclear weapon undoubtedly was based on the foundations laid by Jawaharlal Nehru and enriched by Indira Gandhi. This move was welcomed throughout the world including in the United States and Europe.

The proximity or virtual identity of the attitudes adopted by the non-aligned movement and the socialist countries became very clear during the exchange visits by leaders of the Soviet Union and India, when both countries expressed their concern about the continuing arms race, particularly in the nuclear field, and the mounting danger that it would be extended into outer space. The Delhi Declaration on the principles of a world free of nuclear weapons and violence, adopted on 27 November 1986 at the end of Mr. Gorbachev's official visit to India, testifies to the headway made by the new thought structure that was emerging in response to the needs of an age which was by now both nuclear and cosmic in character. It reflected the firm conviction of both sides that violence had to be abandoned. The Delhi Declaration indeed represented an important stage in the development of a new ethic in international relations.

That gist of India's Action Plan is the elimination of all nuclear weapons in three stages by the year 2010 at the latest. In Stage I the liquidation of short and medium range rocket systems to be followed by a 50 per cent cut in Soviet Union now Russia and US strategic arsenals. All production of nuclear weapons and weapons-grade fissionable material must cease immediately. A moratorium on the testing of nuclear weapons is to be agreed. With immediate effect, to set the stage for the negotiation of an international convention which outlaws the threat or use of such weapons. A moratorium would be imposed on developing, testing and deploying space weapons systems, and the United Nations would evolve a new strategic doctrine of non-provocative defence. Thus, as visualized by Indian diplomacy, a new structure of international relations sustaining a world without nuclear weapons would be based on the principles of co-existence and non-use of force, non-intervention in the internal affairs of other countries, and the right of every state to pursue its own path of development. As Nehru said: "The alternative to co-existence is co-destruction".

So for India the struggle for peace, disarmament, development and independence is indivisible. Only an economically and politically strong community of nations can effectively face the challenge of the nuclear age, only peaceful co-existence can guarantee general progress and development.[2]

Let us refer to the multidimensional foreign policy of India, which was evolved in the 50s and 60s under the leadership of Jawaharlal Nehru in a complex bipolar world, in general and India's stand on weapons of mass destruction in particular.

It was in this period that non-aligned countries, especially India, made a valuable contribution to the lessening of international tension and for creating the necessary atmosphere for peaceful negotiations on the Korean question. The three agonising years of the Korean war gave a new stimulus to the movement for non-alignment which was still in its formative stages. In the United Nations, an Afro-Asian group emerged. The representatives of these countries started consultations and cooperation among themselves on matters of common interest. They also developed fraternal relationship with the socialist countries and some Latin American countries. Jawaharlal Nehru's close colleague, Krishna Menon, played a key role in bringing about this cohesion among the non-aligned countries.

Then came the crisis in Indo-China. The developments in Indochina clearly spotlighted how the struggle for liquidation of colonialism and politics of cold war were getting intertwined. The determination of the United States to encircle the socialist countries and other newly liberated countries with a ring of military bases made the issues crystal clear. It was in recognition of the stand taken and efforts made by the non-aligned countries to put the issues in correct perspective that India was appointed Chairman of the International Commission of Indochina.

The outbreak of the Suez Canal war further cemented the unity of the non-aligned countries. The indignant and united voice of the non-aligned nations, supported by the socialist countries, was largely responsible for saving Egypt from naked aggression.

This may also explain why right from the beginning Jawaharlal Nehru's foreign policy and his concept of non-alignment were bitterly attacked by the United States of America and the Western Power, more especially in 1952, during the period when Dullers appeared on the scene. They regarded the policy assumptions of India as "immoral and short-sighted". US policy makers became bitter about Jawaharlal Nehru's policy of non-alignment and against the steps taken by him to defuse the international tension. The authors of cold war policy not only failed to drag India into bloc entanglements but found in India a country which was rallying many of the newly independent countries to a new order which conflicted with their notions of the division of the world into what they called Free World and "iron curtain countries of the communist world". Notwithstanding all this, the non-aligned movement became a platform for anti-imperialism and anti-colonialism and this firm stand of the movement of a large number of issues brought countries like India closer to the socialist world.

What is of obvious importance in this Declaration is that it demanded an end to any military operation and repressive action against the dependent peoples. The Declaration was carried by 90 votes. Its opponents, nine imperialist powers, did not dare to vote against it and had to be content by simply abstaining.

In the sixties, the policy and practices of neocolonialists took a new turn. While recognising formally the political sovereignty of their former colonies and semi-colonies, they tried to organise military-political blocs. They did not stop short at that. They tried to throttle the independent economic development of these newly freed countries. But these countries had now a new option of taking friendly economic assistance from the Soviet Union on the basis of equality and mutual benefit. This is how the process of close economic cooperation between India and the socialist countries started shaping itself from the fifties onward, though our country did not close its options of cooperation with developed nations like the US and Great Britain.

Notwithstanding a petty-minded tendency among some political leaders to minimise the role of Jawaharlal Nehru in the making of modern

India, there will be no disagreement in any quarter that he was a great patriot. In questioning for ways and means of development and modernisation of India, he always held uppermost the interest of the country and the people. And this quest was concrete and consistent. As early as in 1947, he pointed out that "cooperation between India and Russia will be beneficial to both countries and promote the cause of peace and progress in the world."

In the early period when India had just embarked on the path of consolidating its independence and was engaged in the crucial task of strengthening it, American efforts were directed to inducing the Indian Government to follow a pronouncedly pro-American policy. US Ambassador Henry F. Grady stated on December 7, 1947: "It is tremendously important to keep India on our side in this world struggle."

The United States Defence Department listed two fundamental reasons why India had attracted much attention from the American policy makers at that stage.

"India is important not only because, together with Pakistan, it is about as big as Europe and has tremendously big population, but because its stand on world affairs influences strongly the stand taken by other Asian nations...."

In 1949, another world-shaking event took place with defeat of the American supported Chiang Kaishek regime. This gave a new significance to India in American eyes. This was a period when "more and more Americans tend to look upon India as a stronghold of resistance to the wave of communism sweeping Asia", as Mildred Hughes, Executive Vice-President of the Far East American Council of Commerce and Industry put it.

Jawaharlal Nehru, far-sighted as he was, correctly visualised that Indo-Soviet and Indo-US relations would not develop on the same lines. After the visit of Jawaharlal Nehru towards the end of 1949, an American writer commented that the Indian-American relationship has not yet jelled. The American attitude towards India further reinforced this assessment of Jawaharlal Nehru.

In the early fifties, Indian public opinion was outraged at the ruthless ways of American warfare in Korea. It rightly saw that the American policy in Asia was not a series of isolated and erratic moves but was firmly based upon a pattern of action without any concern for Asian lives or interests. It was in this situation that Nehru again and again pressed the proposal at all national and international forums for a peaceful solution of the conflict in Asia. This stand of Jawaharlal Nehru was described in the American press as "the voice of abnegation" and a policy of "appeasement". Abuse was reinforced by political pressure when India made a request for a loan for wheat purchases. Tom Conolly, Chairman of the Senate Committee on Foreign Relations, made it known on January 25, 1951 that action on the Indian request would be delayed until a sub-committee "looks into the whole question of US relations with India."

When India started openly resisting the American pressure on its relations with People's Republic of China and the question of its admission to the United Nations, she became the target of even more violent American attacks. India's boycott of the Japanese Peace Treaty made the American policy makers resort to harsher steps towards this country. The Americans looked at India's emerging new foreign policy based on independent assessment and sovereignty with disfavour and distrust. On August 28, the New York Daily Mirror accused Nehru of "Asiatic intrigue". What annoyed Washington the most was that "Jawaharlal Nehru is fast becoming one of the great disappointments of the post war era" because he was trying to set up a "third force....suspended in the midair between the two decisive movements of our day–the communism that Russia heads and the democracy of which the United States is the chief champion."

It is pertinent to recapitulate these facts when foundations for India's independent foreign policy were being evolved by Jawaharlal Nehru, for more than one reason. During the last four to five decades certain basic changes have taken place in the international situation and corelations of the forces.

Leaders are not "born" in political societies, they are "made". They get identified, define their own ends and means with precision, and achieve the capacity to direct the opinions of others only to the extent they can react rationally and emotionally to the needs, demands, hopes and decision of the largest number of individuals in any given political society. This is not true merely of the contemporary democratic political orders and States. The "born" leaders died as soon as human beings left their caves behind and started living communally. Even in the most ancient "community"—however small—argument, and agreement and mitigation, at least among the largest possible number of individuals, replaced the capacity for arbitrary violence as the weapons of the leaders. This applies even to the cases of such freak phenomena as the Napoleons and the Hitlers, of human society's 6000 years long "political" history. Such individuals invariably became ineffective and failed as soon as their own or their immediate clique's subjective desires and assessments became the predominant motive forces of policies and programmes. This is also true of leaders who try to act within frameworks of democracy, consultation and concession. Neville Chamberlain and Winston Churchill, Eisenhower and Lyndon Johnson, the "liberal" leaders who rejected Mahatma Gandhi in the second and third decades of this century, are pitiful examples of brilliantly intelligent leaders failing because they could not understand or would not accept the challenge thrown to them by quick, qualitative changes in public opinion which may not always be quickly logical, but is always instinctively correct in its assessment of the future.

The decisive element in successful political leadership has always been the capacity to sense moments of drastic change in the opinions and emotions of the largest number of politically aware individuals in the given society, and be sincerely in tune with them. This capacity cannot be acquired by the "pragmatist" or the opportunist except in the very short run.

This shows that in the final analysis it is the people, their aspirations and how they assert themselves which determined the fate of the leaders. It is this single factor which gave a unique place to Jawaharlal Nehru in Indian history. He had in fact a prophetic mind. He could perceive as early as in the mid-50s how the threat of weapons of mass destruction threaten the existence of humanity on our planet. Therefore, his main endeavour was to rouse the people all over the world, in India in particular against these weapons of mass destruction.

He, however, openly expressed the apprehension that certain nuclear power countries may monopolise the use of atomic energy and deny other countries to harness this potential for the well-being of the people.

Nuclear Weapons and Nehru's Vision

That after 44 years the world is facing almost an identical problem shows how Jawaharlal Nehru could visualise the turbulent days ahead for the developing countries. It is precisely this what we are witnessing today. And it was this danger which he foresaw.

We reproduce here some of the excerpts from his historic speech in the House of the People (Lok Sabha), May 10, 1954.

"Honourable Members on both sides of the House have talked about banning nuclear weapons. But it is not quite clear to me how our sentiments or a strong speech in this House will lead to such a ban. There is no doubt that these weapons will ultimately have to be controlled, if not put an end to. But, from what we know of this world, who is to bell the cat? It might have been possible if there had been no conflict between the colossi in this respect. Neither of them is going to control the nuclear bomb till he is certain that the other will control it. Each will sit back and say to himself that despite some public protestation, there will really be no attempt to control the weapons. Yet it is necessary to control them. The question remains how to do it. International law, as is well known, is too feeble an instrument yet to achieve it."

He further said when the United States acquired atomic bombs "that the human mind and human efforts are unleashing tremendous powers without quite knowing how to control them. They cannot be controlled by a mere desire or demand for banning them. Nobody can really control the human mind from going on unleashing new forces. One of the political problems of the day is how to approach this problem of control which is of vital consequences. Such an approach presupposes some measure of lessening of tension in the world, some measure of mutual confidence on the part of the great nations, some agreement to allow each country to live its own life. The only alternative is conflict, and if the idea of conflict is in the minds of nations then the atom bomb will undoubtedly remain."

He, however, clearly perceived that "it is perfectly clear that atomic energy can be used for peaceful purposes to the immense advantage of humanity. It may take some years before it can be used more or less economically.... the use of atomic energy for peaceful purposes is far more important for a country like India whose power resources are limited, therefore a country like France, an industrially advanced country. Take the United States of America, which already has vast power resources of other kinds. To have an additional source of power like atomic energy does not mean very much for them. No doubt they can use it; but it is not so indispensable for them as for a power-starved or power-hungry country like India or like most of the other countries in Asia and Africa."

He went out of his way to highlight that "it would be to the disadvantage of a country like India if that is restricted or stopped. We should remember this very important aspect of the so-called international control".

"Who is to control atomic energy internationally? Who are the nations that are going to control it? One may say, the United Nations. Obviously, there is no other organization approaching the United Nations in its international jurisdiction. And yet, the House knows, the United Nations as it is does not include in its scope even the big nations of the world. Some of the biggest are kept out. The United Nations can control only itself. It cannot control any nation which is not in it, which it refuses to admit and with which it would not have anything to do. The result will be that though it may control a great part of the world, still there is a part of the world which is not controlled by it. That part over which there is no control, may make all the mischief. Therefore, the question of international control become difficult. Reference has been made to international control in President Eisenhower's speech. We all agree with the proposition that there should be proper international control and proper use made of the stock of fissile materials, so that all countries can use them for research work or for proper purposes. But how is this to be done? That is where the difficulty comes in.

President Eisenhower refers to some agency of the United Nations. That appears reasonable but let us see what actual proposals have been made in regard to atomic energy control by various countries. At the beginning of the year, the United States said: "An international control agency shall be set up by the United Nations. It shall thereafter be an independent body outside the control of the Security Council and of the United Nations. The United Nations is merely supposed to set up the agency and wash its hands of it. It becomes an independent organization. This organization will, of course, have an unlimited right of inspection..... It shall have the right to maintain its own guards on the territory of any foreign state, licensed to engage in any of the processes of the production of or research in atomic energy. Thus the atomic energy body becomes a super-State, maintaining its own guards or armies or whatever you like to call them. Then again, it shall own and control–mark these words—the raw materials mined, the plants in which the ore is processed, and all plants which deal with production of atomic energy wherever they may be situated in any country of the world. This is a very far-reaching provision. It means that all our raw materials and our mines would be owned and controlled by that independent body which is even independent of the United Nations after it is created. It means tremendous power being concentrated in the hands of a select body. It shall decide if, when and where and to what extent the various processes may be carried out and in which parts of the world atomic energy plants may be established—and there are limitations also and it shall have authority to issue or withhold licenses from countries, institutions or enterprises engaged in any activities relating to the production of atomic energy."

Jawaharlal Nehru did not mince matters. He warned that "the Great Powers" will "lord over" the policies of the various nations engaged in peaceful uses of the atomic energy. He did not leave it at that. He said :

"I say with all the respect to them (Great Powers) that they will have grip over all the atomic energy areas and raw materials in every country."

"Now for a country like India is it a desirable prospect?" He asked.

This graphically shows that what India is witnessing today was in the mind of Jawaharlal Nahru. That also explains why he gave a top priority to building nuclear technology and initiated a series of measures, which have enabled the country to reach the present level of development of technology both in atomic and space areas.

The importance with which Science and Technology (S&T) is viewed in the economic growth and development of the country owes a great deal to the vision and foresight of India's first Prime Minister, Jawaharlal Nehru who had implicit faith in the application of modern science for the alleviation of most of the ills in society, and the betterment of humankind. In this endeavour he encouraged the growth of science and technology, and provided the inputs for the establishment and expansion of both civilian and defence scientific laboratories and establishments within the country. Amongst his inner circle of advisors could be counted the leaders of Indian science at the time Dr. Homi Bhabha of nuclear science, Sir Shanti Swarup Bhatnagar, and his successor as Director General of the Council of Scientific and Industrial Research (CSIR) Professor M.S.Thacker, and Dr. Daulat Singh Kothari, the first Scientific Advisor to the Minister for Defence as already mentioned in this study.

Over the years, India's total scientific and technological strength has grown to some 40 lakhs personnel, and well over a hundred laboratories and establishments spread throughout the country. India is often considered to possess the third largest pool of scientists and engineers in the world.[3]

It is this edifice built by Nehru, later consolidated by Indira Gandhi and Rajiv Gandhi, which has enabled India to become self-reliant in science and technology and in atomic energy and space in particular. One cannot erase this fact of history.

REFERENCES

1. *A Place in History*, M. Chalapathi Rao: Jawaharlal Nehru: Life and Work, pp. 26-27, 29.
2. *Jawaharlal Nehru and the Foreign Policy of India*, Jan Filipsky: pp. 3-9.
3. *Asian Strategic Review*: 1994-95: Rahul Roy Chowdhary: pp. 224-25.

14

Humanisation and Democratisation of International Relations

Hiroshima and Nagasaki, the first victims of the atomic bomb, the use of chemical and biological weapons in Vietnam in the late 60s and early 70s, the tragic developments during the Gulf War in 1991 in which thousands of people both the American armed forces and Arab peoples became victims of chemical and biological weapons—if all these developments are pieced together it becomes abundantly clear that weapons of mass destruction are no more in the military force of the powers that possess them. They have been used with vengeance to achieve certain political objectives.

On December 19, 1945 President Truman said: "Whether we like it or not we must recognize that the victory which we have Uron in the Second World War has placed upon the American people the continuing burden of responsibility of world leadership."

Commenting on a statement made by Reagan on June 2, 1982, prior to his departure for Europe, the *Washington Post* noted: "Reagan described his mission as carrying on the task of world leadership." This country never sought but had been thrust upon it at the end of World War II.

This shows that the running threat behind the mass killing of the civilians during all these three events was the political ambition of the US to establish its leadership over the world.

Till the demise of the Soviet Union a myth of the "Soviet threat" or danger of "Communist menace" was built up to justify the use of these weapons of mass destruction. And now a new ideological cover has been evolved, that is, to build "democratic systems in various countries based on market economy." This is no place to evaluate these myths. Perhaps the people all over the world, the developing and the underdeveloped countries through their own experience have begun to see the real motivation behind the use of weapons of mass destruction either directly or as "weapons of deterrence". Let us leave this question at that.

This study has clearly established that in the 80s the US violated the 1972 Biological Weapon Convention by supplying Iraq with different biological components for production of chemical weapons. But there is something more to it. The delivery to Iraq of biological material as established in this study by the US confirms that it has violated the Biological Weapon Convention. Moreover, after February 1989, it acted against the letter and spirit of Anti-Terrorist Act adopted by the US.

This study also shows that the Administration of the US approved of the delivery to Iraq of biological material and technology of dual use during the first Gulf War, the Iran–Iraq War. The motivation was clear. The objective was that the intensity of Iran–Iraq War should get a new dimension. However, when the Gulf War syndrome began to adversely effect the health of American armed forces and their families, this fact was either underplayed or concealed from the common Americans people.

All these facts now have become public after the Report of Senate Committee on US Chemical and Biological Weapons Related Dual Use Exported to Iraq. This report speaks for itself and needs no elaboration. Nevertheless, what the international community has to understand is that weapons of mass destruction, biological, chemical and nuclear—no more merely threaten the existence of human race on our planet. They are already being used though on a limited scale. In this sense annihilation of human race comes on the immediate agenda. It is no more a theoretical question. The danger is real though it is not being fully comprehended by the people all over the world. Thus the question of humanisation and democratisation of international relations have become a key link for the very survival of human race.

Taking a general view of international relations as they have developed from ancient times to this day, we can see that they form continuous chain of conflicts, wars, international animosity, confrontation and bloodshed claiming heavy tolls of many hundreds of millions of human lives, not to speak of the destruction of numberless material and cultural values. The question, naturally, arises: are such notions as democratisation and humanisation generally applicable to them, and if they are, then to what extent? Is it not a far-fetched attempt, yet another illusion or a desire that cannot be achieved? If humanity has so far failed to humanise and democratise relations between nations, are there any grounds to hope and trust that it will be able to do so in the future?

These are no simple questions. Yet, we would not call the combination of international relations with the idea of their democratisation and humanisation an extremely illusory and absolutely untenable matter. It is consonant with, is rooted in, and is substantiated by, the imperishable dream of humanity about universal fraternity, love and unity.

But this is the way the world is arranged: in order to appreciate the intransient value of human personality, rivers of blood had to be shed; in order to understand that men are brethren, ages of enmity had to be lived; in order to see the absurdity of war, the brink of self-destruction had to be approached. Willy-nilly, all this brings one to a sad conclusion that the possibility of a positive development becomes real only when the possibilities of a negative development have been exhausted. Today, they have been largely exhausted. That is why to pose today the issue of humanising and democratising international relations is to meet an urgent moral need.

Nuclear Cosmic Era

In the last quarter of the present century, a number of worlddevelopment trends have surfaced clearly enough to make the idea of democratising and humanising international relations an imperative. First of all, the special context of the nuclear–cosmic era that it is fraught with the possibility of self-destruction of civilisation. The situation is further compounded by use of biological and chemical weapons as we have seen in this study. It is also the ascending tendency to closer interdependence of states in all spheres of their relations—economic, political, military–strategic, ecological and humanitarian. Lastly, it is the aggravation of the so-called global problems which have undermined man's confidence in his supremacy over Nature and his unlimited possibilities to draw from it.

At the close of the 20th century, mankind has come face to face with the grave questions: will it be able to cope with forces of destruction which mankind itself has brought to life, will it find strength to remove the threat of nuclear cataclysm, putting an end to the unchecked arms race, the contamination of the environment and setting limits to the irrational squandering of natural resources?

Already today these processes trigger off numerous crises—material, raw material, energy, and food crises and spiritual, the crises of ideals, morals and hopes. Not only do they create a real threat to the survival of humanity as a race, but to its security—political, social, economic, legal and ecological. Not infrequently they deprive man of an adequate notion of his place in the modern and constantly changing society, estranging him from the surrounding world with its values, and instill in his mind negative and often wrong stereotypes, prejudices, and distorted perceptions of realities. As a result, the sway of the established stereotypes of thinking and behaviour prevents man from looking critically at the world and at himself. In our view, this is one of the reasons why man steadily loses his ability to draw lessons from the past and the present, from social and political crises now and then upheaving society, to check them. They remain beyond his comprehension, and, consequently, beyond his power; they loom over him as a fatal doom. The outstanding humanist writer Berthold Brecht wrote once that as long as masses remain object of politics, they perceive everything that happens to them not as an experience, but as fate; catastrophes teach them nothing—a guinea-pig will never learn biology. And man will remain the object, the guinea-pig , as long as he is estranged from politics and economics, from making political decisions, as long as he serves as a means, representing a relative value, not an absolute one.

For that reason, ridding man of prejudices that have piled up is a major humanitarian task of our time. What we need today is to free information flows from stereotypes making up "the image of the enemy", from bias, prejudices and absurd fiction, from the preconceived distortion or emasculation of the truth. There is a political elite in the developed countries, which lives in the past. It is aspiring for "world leadership".

This is an indisputable imperative of the contemporary world, which, in addition to its growing integrity and a closer interdependence of states and nations, is characterised by a deep political and ideological split of humanity. These two, seemingly little compatible but at once real sides of the single world process, give birth to fresh contradictions and conflicts, which in the long run, have brought the world to the brink of non-existence.

The threat of self-destruction looming large over humanity and the resultant unnatural situation of the apocalyptic adaptation to the possible nuclear cataclysm, cannot but leave their imprint on the mentality and behaviour of people, their morals and whole way of life. Such phenomena as social passivity, scepticism, indifference, corrosion of supreme moral ideals, depravity, the increasingly more rife crimes, violence, drug-addiction and alcoholism, also largely derive from man's lack of confidence in their own future and the future of their children. And this refers to all societies without exception.

Universal Human Problems

This circumstance indicates that the humanisation and democratisation of contemporary international relations is not a partial or local problem. It can rightly and fully be included into the category of universal human problems, for it reflects the truly human aspect, placing man in the focus of attention. It is an immediate derivative of common human interests in preserving peace and preventing a nuclear missile war. It is precisely the threat of war and destruction of life on earth that has today placed all people irrespective of their national, racial, social or class affinity in no other position than that of being hostages, of biological, chemical and above all nuclear weapons and has given birth to the unity of their common interests; it is this threat that began to wash away the wall between the socially opposite societies, which proved equally susceptible and vulnerable both to nuclear holocaust and to other negative processes inherent in the contemporary world.

Thus, the threat to human survival demonstrated for all to see not only the extent of the interdependence of the modern world, it also demonstrated that humanisation and democratisation are just as interconnected and inseparable as peace and security are. More than that, they are indissolubly linked up with the problem of securing universal peace. It is hardly right to speak today of a selective humanisation, a humanisation confined to a limited space, a separate region or to bilateral relations. Humanisation will be real only taken as an all-embracing stream, as a single world process engulfing all countries and all peoples. There can be no isolated oasis of humanism if the world around them is dehumanised, just as there can be no isolated islets of security in the perilous ocean of enmity and hatred. Many outstanding leaders of the world including Gandhi, Jawaharlal Nehru were the first to articulate this concept of one world.

The world of today is saturated with political, ideological and other controversies so densely and is characterised by such different concepts of human rights, morality and ethics arising from fundamentally different world outlooks, that the questions naturally arises: how to dovetail democratic and humanitarian principles with real social processes going on in it, with its contradictions and collisions, specific social, economic and political struggles, with confrontation of different, often opposite interests of people and states and its division into military-political alliances and groupings?

Before attempting to give an answer to that question, we shall expound our own understanding of the humanisation and democratisation of international relations. First of all, it should be noted that the two components of that notion correlate with each other as an end and a means, where the end is humanisation and the means of achieving it, democratisation. On the more general plane, the humanisation of international relations implies, in our view, a process of their gradual transformation from relations dividing people into relations uniting them, into relations promoting the interests of man as such and irrespective of his national, political, social or class affinity, promoting also his material, spiritual and moral development perfection; into relations in which it is man, not state or other economic and political mechanisms and institutions, comes forward as the measure of all things.

As to the democratisation of international relations, it should be based on principles of the peaceful coexistence of states, which presupposes the indispensable rules of international cooperation, such as recognition of sovereignty and independence of states, their equality, non-interference into the home affairs of each other, refusal to impose from outside–no matter by what means—social systems, way of life, policies, in other words, the freedom for each people for each state to choose its own road.

Solution of problems of democratisation and humanisation depends both on man himself and the objective conditions in which he lives and operates. If man draws all his knowledge, sensation, etc. from the world of the senses and the experience gained through it, then what has to be done is to arrange the empirical world in such a way that man experiences and becomes accustomed to what is truly human in it and that he becomes aware of himself as man. If correctly understood interest is the principle of all morality, man's private interest must be made to coincide with the interest of humanity... If man is shaped by environment, his environment must be made human.

In other words, a dual task should be accomplished: to humanise man and at the same time to change the world to conform to the nature of man who has been made human. However, despite repeated attempts, man has not so far succeeded in accomplishing that task. Furthermore, the great humanitarian ideas of many social revolutions which were most strikingly embodied in the watchwords of the glorious French Revolution-liberty, equality and fraternity—turned, with the passage of time, into their opposites.

What is happening is that as mankind masters nature, man seems to become enslaved to other man or to his own infamy. Even the pure light of science seems unable to shine but on the dark background of ignorance. All our invention and progress seem to result in endowing material forces with intellectual life, and in stultifying human life into a material force. This dehumanises both man and societies, the political elite in particular. The issue of making man more human, of turning him from a means of social development he has been transformed into a machine without soul and spirit. Media, particularly electronic media, has been transformed into a massive "mind management machinery". Instead of rousing healthy instincts of man, it not only promotes consumerism but fans inhuman tendencies. Thus those who control mind management machinery have a vested interest in dehumanising the consciousness of man. This is how animosities, hatred, religious and ethnic conflicts are made part of the consciousness of man. This makes a commonman passive spectator.

But it has long been known that there is an indissoluble connection between the end and the means, and for that reason the result is inseparable from the way and the method of its attainment. It is not the result that is the real whole.

Incidentally, the great humanists of the past never doubted that the edifice of human happiness cannot be erected with the aid of violence, that a particular act of injustice cannot be removed using another act of injustice, that the happiness of some should not be based on the unhappiness of others, that good cannot be enforced.

But ages of errors and misconceptions notwithstanding man to this day operates using the same methods: he strives to ensure peace and strengthen universal security by means of violence. And here again a question inevitable arises: is the practice of upholding and ensuring peace in inter-state relations by proxy of weapons justifiable from the humanist point of view, can the realisation of the essentially humanist end by anti-humanist, and, consequently, amoral means be justified?

Humanism and Morality

Humanism is inseparable from morality. Faith in the possibility of humanising international relations can only be guaranteed if policy is governed by morality. Today the moral side of the activity of states in the international arena cannot but cause anxiety. Estrangement always generally inherent in the foreign policy of states, which in their activities were largely guided by egoistic, exclusively national interests and which based relations amongst themselves on the balance of forces. This estrangement still persists, its traditional manifestations having been replenished with a fresh one—the division of the world into different socio-economic systems, and consequently, into states belonging to any one of them. This division has long been made an absolute, it was considered to have a self-contained significance. The thesis became predominant the international relations constituted a sphere of influence which should decide who will win? All this had led to an unprecedented confrontation in the world, which, it seemed, left no place for humanism or democracy. Relations between states were reduced to brinkmanship, to brandishing with nuclear missiles accompanied by an unbridled arms race. The tough confrontation of the military-political groupings found expression in their prolonged inability and unwillingness to look for and find alternative ways of developing international relations, seeking reasonable compromises in settling issues of vital significance for the world. More than that, this confrontation had finally led to a situation in which the whole world has become its hostage. Essentially, this train of events meant the triumph of politics over morality, the triumph of narrow national interests over universal human interests, it signified the renunciation of the idea of making international relations more humane.

After the demise of the Soviet Union, the situation did not change. Now new power centres are being created and the concept of "leadership" has re-emerged with vigour.

However, the practical task of combining politics and morality, which had been separated from each other for such a long time has become more relevant today than ever before.

To sum up, it may be said that the possibility of permeating international relations with ideas of humanism and democracy is quite realistic. For it is based on new opportunities that have opened up today to establish a fruitful cooperation between states. This is also corroborated by the increasing recognition by various states of the concept of peaceful coexistence, their greater interdependence and wider cooperation in ever new areas and along ever new lines. This implies that, it is inadmissible to contaminate the sphere of cooperation with differences.

World Leadership

New concepts of "leadership of the world, democracy based on market economy", imposing Western models on developing societies and all such ideas are holding back the process of building international relations based on humanism.

This, in turn, presupposes the deideologisation of foreign policies and inter-state relations. What we mean by this is the renunciation of outdated ideas, ideological stereotypes, myths, notions and approaches that have outlived their time and which run counter to the real interests of states and nations, aggravate inter-state relations, make absolute ideological differences and mould the confrontation-like way of thinking and action in the international arena. The developments in the post-cold war period confirm this conclusion.

In a word, deideologisation means a refusal to see the world through the prism of "world leadership," and, thereby, the rejection of the rigid alternative of the all-or-nothing type; it signifies a refusal to impose on the world one's own exclusive values, one's own way of thinking and of life; it calls for recognising the pluralistic nature of the world, the multiformity of varying and differing interests, freedom of every human being to take the road of its own choice; it presupposes a balance of interests as the basis of interrelations between states. In other words, deideologisation paves the way to the true democratisation and humanisation of international relations, making them civilised and directing them to people's good and prosperity.

To resolve this task is not so simple. What is needed here is prolonged and persistent work, steadily breaking down outdated relations on the basis of new realities. For this real prerequisites have sprung in modern international relations. And if joint efforts result in their realisation, the prospects for making international relations more humane will become real, with reason, knowledge, and moral principles, rather than selfish ambitions and prejudices. This will motivate various states in resolving numerous contradictions in the world and achieving a balance of interests.

Humanity repeatedly tackled the problem of how to humanise and democratise international relations in the person of its finest representatives. Understandably, the very idea has not arisen from scratch. It has been derived from the already amassed experience of peaceful and non-peaceful coexistence of states and is based on the generally recognised human values, on the age-long strivings of man for peace. At all times, that idea had its supporters and followers, its heroic defenders and martyrs. It inspired many humanists and enlighteners of the past—Erasme, Grotius, Saint Pierre, Rousseau, Kant, etc. But under the undivided sway of the principle of force in international relations and the priority of the narrow national interests of states, in conditions of antagonism and confrontation between them, all plans to remake interstate relations, embodying in them the idea of eternal peace, could not but be utopian.

New realities have arisen today in the world: having entered the nuclear age and having created weapons of mass destruction, mankind has thereby deprived itself of mortality. If formerly wars claimed millions of lives, annihilating whole nations, their atrocities and ravages notwithstanding, did not threat humanity with perishing as a race. Today if nuclear war were to break out, all life on earth would be killed. To this we shall add the following: development of conventional war material has reached such a point, that even a non-nuclear war can be readily compared with a nuclear one in terms of its fatal aftermaths, furthermore, one should reckon with the existence of a network of nuclear power stations, whose destruction is tantamount to the use of nuclear weapons. Expansion of communications, modern transportation means, creation of mass-destruction weapons together with the means of their delivery making it possible for them to reach any point of earth in counted minutes—all this has strikingly revealed how small and crowded our planet is, how limited is the space occupied by humanity, and how vulnerable it is not only to nuclear, but also to conventional war. There is only one road for it, the road of peaceful democratic development, the road of cooperation of all states with the aim of turning our planet into a proper place for human habitation.

The entire historical experience and the experience of practical policies from times immemorial to our day show that to safeguard its own security against outside threats has always been a major task of the state. The very same experience demonstrates that so far the world community has not worked out for this any other mechanism than the maintenance of the military-political balance, the balance of forces, the military-political parity, etc. But this mechanism, is in turn, inseparable from the arms race and militarism.

How, then, to break out of this vicious circle?

The way out lies through a succession of consistent steps in the field of disarmament, but this will be the beginning of the process.

The world is witnessing a new process which is connected with objective world processes in the sphere of economic, scientific and technological ties and interstate relations and which leads to a stronger interdependence of states in the political, economic and military-strategic fields. Interdependence gives birth to common interests, while the latter lays the foundation for political agreements and the rapprochement of states. It is precisely thanks to the development of economic ties, to processes of integration and the growing awareness of the existence of global problems that common human interests are being shaped. And a development taking cognisance of trends towards internationalisation of production, the processes of integration going on in the various parts of the world, lead, in turn, to the emergence of new types of interrelations between states. In the framework of integrational unions, war as a means of politics is essentially ruled out. This is exemplified by integrational unions of today, above all by the European Community—an organisation much advanced along the road of economic and political integration. We believe that there are certain grounds to consider such unions as the rudiments, even as a prototype of the future world confederation of states, the more so that today a trend becomes discernable (although not so strikingly apparent, but still quite noticeable) towards a gradual coming closer together and a gradual merger of integrational unions themselves, towards removing partitions separating them. In other words, processes of integration change fundamentally "international mentality".

It should be pointed out that the idea of integration as a real basis for peoples to come closer together and unite as the main road to achieve peace is gaining an ever greater currency and recognition in the various circles of the world public. And, indeed, without such a rapprochement, the projects to readjust the world and create a new world order, the plans to democratise and humanise international relations, become essentially abortive.

Democratisation and humanisation of international relations is not a single act, it is a prolonged process having both remote, ideal aims, and immediate, practical aims that can be realised in the foreseeable future, forming, as it were, "small bricks" which would help to erect the edifice of the future humanised human civilisation. The first and most urgent of such tasks is the task to eliminate the threat of nuclear war, create the system of an all-embracing security based on the principles of peaceful coexistence, to strengthen trust between states through surmounting the confrontation-like way of thinking and action, to introduce the rules of civilised behaviour and openness in international relations, enhancing the role of public, peoples diplomacy.

This study shows that in the end of the present century two parallel developments are shaping themselves.

Firstly, there is a marked tendency in Europe which coincides with the new realities on the global plane. The most outstanding feature of this tendency is growing cooperation among the various sates. This tendency is gaining momentum in Europe. This implies that the most developed nations have evolved their own path in the new historical conditions.

Secondly, the developing and underdeveloped nations and some of the erstwhile socialist countries of Central and East Europe are witnessing serious difficulties in the nation-state building process. Some of these states are afflicted with ethnic conflicts and face the challenge of their disintegration. Third party's intervention has created new complications. Similar problems have surfaced in some of the African and Asian countries.

However, what is most disturbing aspect of the present international atmosphere is that the concept of "World Leadership" or, to put it differently, the "hegemonistic" ambitions of some developed nations, the United States in particular instead of being curbed have begun to assert themselves, though along with a new concept of "sharing leadership" too has surfaced. But it conceals more than what it reveals. There are some states which are being encouraged to become nuclear weapon powers and this goes unnoticed. Israel stands as a glaring example of this.

What is a more disturbing aspect of this parallel development is that weapons of mass destruction are being used as a political weapon to drive a wedge between some countries. The way Iraq was supplied technology and raw material to build stockpiles of biological and chemical weapons that too contrary to all international norms is indeed revealing though this Arab country has now to pay a heavy price for not playing the game assigned to it. Again India's nuclear tests alarmed the United States and some other nations.

This confirms the conclusion that the road to build a non-violent world, free from all weapons of mass destruction, nuclear in particular, will not be smooth. It would rather be a difficult road. Jawaharlal Nehru visualised this long time back. Nevertheless in the final analysis, people on our planet will assert themselves, sooner to later, including the Americans.

This is how an American writer Carl Oglesby has summed up the mood of peace-loving Americans:

"The long road to international morality leads through the creation of international order, and international order necessitates, first of all, the creation of international stability. We can only create international stability if all the major powers in the world accept that the principle that in the nuclear age no side can change the political status quo through the use of force and through direct challenge to another side ...The Soviets learnt that lesson more painfully in Cuba. That lesson is still to be learnt in many parts of the world, but I believe that the cause of peace, the cause of global reconciliation, the cause of international adjustment, requires, first, the creation of stability, and stability in Asia will not be achieved by American intervention."

This statement speaks for itself and needs to comments. The moral is that objective Americans are no longer passive spectators in the struggle for humanisation and democratisation of the international order. Today their voice may be feeble. Tomorrow it may turn into an avalanche.

This also leads us to the following two conclusions as far as India is concerned.

Firstly, India being the biggest democratic country of the world has to uphold the banner of humanisation and democratisation of international relations in keeping with the tradition of Indian culture and its national movement.

Secondly, India has to come to grip with the present realities of the world and evolve politico-economic and geopolitical strategies to defend its sovereignty, independence and security.

INDEX